Anonymous

The Columbian Songster

Containing a Collection of the most admired New, Favourite and Patriotic Songs

Anonymous

The Columbian Songster
Containing a Collection of the most admired New, Favourite and Patriotic Songs

ISBN/EAN: 9783337307080

Printed in Europe, USA, Canada, Australia, Japan

Cover: Foto ©Thomas Meinert / pixelio.de

More available books at **www.hansebooks.com**

SONG.

MY sweet pretty Mog, you're as soft as a bog,
And wild as a kitten, and wild as a kitten,
Those eyes in your face—(O pity my case)
Poor Dermot hath smitten, poor Dermot hath smitten.
For softer than silk, and as fair as new milk,
Your lilly white hand is, your lilly white hand is:
Your shape's like a pail, from your head to your tail,
You're strait as a wand is, you're strait as a wand is.

Your lips red as cherries, and your curling hair is
As black as the devil, as black as the devil:
Your breath is as sweet, too, as any potatoe,
Or orange from Seville, or orange from Seville.
When dress'd in your boddice, you trip like a goddess,
So nimbly, so frisky; so nimbly, so frisky:
A kiss on your cheek, 'tis so soft and so sleek,
Would warm me like whisky, would warm me like
        whisky;

I grunt and I pine, and sob like a swine,
Because you're so cruel, because you're so cruel:
No rest can I take, and asleep or awake
I dream of my jewel, I dream of my jewel.
Your hate then give over, nor Dermot your lover
So cruelly handle, so cruelly handle!
Or Dermot must die, like a pig in a stye,
Or snuff of a candle, or snuff of a candle.

You shall be my Love.

AS Jockey sat beneath a shade,
   While breezes fan the grove,
Young Jenny tript along the mead,
   The lass that Jockey lov'd:
O! did you know, he cry'd, the pain
   That harbours in my breast,
You ne'er would let me sue in vain,
   But make me ever blest.
      Then lets gang down the burn so gay,
         Or thro' the shady grove,
      For there we'll toy and kiss and play,
         And you shall be my love.

For I'll no longer single be,
　I hate a single life;
Then Jenny do incline to me,
　And thou shalt be my wife:
For Oh! your een they glitter so,
　Their charms I scarce can teel,
But this I know, where'er I go,
　I love my Jenny weel.
　　　Then let's gang down, &c.

Young Jenny heard the tender tale,
　And promis'd to be kind;
Soft tales of love did soon prevail,
　And soon she own'd her mind:
Next day to kirk they fondly stray'd,
　There vow'd to love for life,
Fair Jane, tho' late the coldest maid,
　Is now the fondest wife.
　　　They now gang down the burn so gay,
　　　　Or thro' the shady grove,
　　　And there they toy and kiss and play,
　　　　Exchanging vows of love.

The Banks of the Banna.

SHEPHERDS I have lost my love,
　Have you seen my Anna?
Pride of every shady grove,
　Upon the banks of Banna.

I for her my home forsook,
　Near yon misty mountain,
Left my flock, my pipe, my crook,
　Greenwood shade and fountain.

Never shall I see them more
　Until her returning;
All the joys of life are o'er,
　From gladness chang'd to mourning.
Whither is my charmer flown!
　Shepherds tell me whither!
Ah! woe's me, perhaps she's gone
　For ever and for ever.

The Banks of the Dee.

IT was summer so softly the breezes were blowing,
   And sweetly the nightingale sung from a tree,
At the foot of the rock, when the river was flowing,
   I sat myself down on the banks of the Dee.

Flow on, lovely Dee, flow on, thou sweet river,
   Thy bank's purest streams shall be dear to me ever,
'Twas there I first gain'd the affection and favor
   Of Jamie, the glory and pride of the Dee.

But now he's gone from me, and left me thus mourn-
   To quell the proud Spaniards, so valient is he; [ing,
And yet there's no hope of his speedy returning,
   To wander again on the banks of the Dee.

He's gone, hapless youth, o'er the loud roaring billows,
   The sweetest and kindest of all his brave fellows,
And has left me to mourn amongst these green willows,
   The lonesomest maid on the banks of the Dee.

But time and my prayers may perhaps yet restore him,
   Blest peace may restore the dear shepherd to me;
And when he comes home, with such care I'll watch
     o'er him,
   He never shall quit the sweet banks of the Dee.

The Dee then shall flow, all its beauties displaying,
   The lambs on its banks shall again be seen playing,
Whilst I with my Jamie am carelessly straying,
   And tasting again all the sweets of the Dee.

The Dusky Night.

THE dusky night rides down the sky,
   And ushers in the morn,
The hounds all join in jovial cry,
   The huntsman winds his horn.
     And a hunting we will go, &c.

The wife around her husband throws
   Her arms to make him stay,
My dear it rains, it hails, it blows,
   You cannot hunt to-day.
     Yet a hunting, &c.

Sly Reynard now like light'ning flies,
  And sweeps across the vale,
But when the hounds too near he spies,
  He drops his bushy tail.
    Then a hunting, &c.

Fond echo seems to like the sport,
  And join the jovial cry,
The woods and hills the sound retort,
  And music fills the sky,
    When a hunting, &c.

At last his strength to faintness worn,
  Poor Reynard ceases flight;
Then hungry homeward we return
  To feast away the night.
    And a drinking, &c.

Ye jovial hunters in the morn
  Prepare then for the chace,
Rise at the sounding of the horn,
  And health with sport embrace,
    When a hunting, &c.

Too plain, dear Youth.

TOO plain, dear youth, these tell-tale eyes
  My heart your own declare;
But for heaven sake let it suffice
  You reign triumphant there.

Forbear your utmost power to try,
  Nor further urge your sway;
Press not for what I must deny,
  For fear I should obey.

Could all your arts successful prove,
  Would you a maid undo,
Whose greatest failing is her love,
  And that her love for you?

Say, would you use that very power
  You from her fondness claim,
To ruin in one fatal hour
  A life of spotless fame?

Resolve not then to do an ill,
  Because perhaps you may,
But rather use your utmost skill
  To save me than betray.

Be you yourself my virtue's guard,
  Defend and not pursue,
Since 'tis a task for me too hard
  To strive with love and you.

The Miller's Wedding.

LEAVE, neighbours, your work, and to sport and to play;
Let the tabor strike up, and the village be gay;
No day thro' the year shall more cheerful be seen,
For Ralph of the Mill marries Sue of the Green.

CHORUS.

I love Sue, and Sue loves me,
And while the wind blows,
And while the mill goes,
Who'll be so happy, so happy as we!

Let lords and fine folks, who for wealth take a bride,
Be marry'd to day, and to-morrow be cloy'd;
My body is stout, and my heart is as sound,
And my love, like my courage, will never give ground.
  Chorus—I love Sue, &c.

Let ladies of fashion the best jointures wed,
And prudently take the best bidders bed;
Such signing and sealing's no part of our bliss,
We settle our hearts, and we seal with a kiss.
  Chorus—I love Sue, &c.

Tho' Ralph is not courtly, nor none of your beaux,
Nor bounces, nor flatters, nor wears your fine cloaths,
In nothing he'll follow the folks of high life,
Nor e'er turn his back on his friend or his wife.
  Chorus—I love Sue, &c.

While thus I am able to work at my mill,
While thus thou art kind, and thy tongue but lies still,

Our joys shall continue, and ever be new,
And none be so happy as Ralph and his Sue.
Chorus—I love Sue, &c.

The Sailor's Farewell.

THE topsail shivers in the wind,
  The ship she's cast to sea;
But yet my soul, my heart, my mind,
  Are, Mary, moor'd with thee;
For though thy sailor's bound afar,
Still love shall be his leading star.

Should landmen flatter when we're sail'd,
  O doubt their artful tales;
No gallant sailor ever fail'd,
  But Cupid fill'd his sails;
Thou art the compass of my soul,
Which steers my heart from pole to pole.

Syrens in every port we meet,
  More fell than rocks and waves;
But sailors of the valiant fleet,
  Are lovers, and not slaves:
No foes our courage shall subdue,
Altho' we've left our hearts with you.

These are our cares; but if you're kind,
  We'll scorn the dashing main,
The rocks, the billows, and the wind,
  The powers of *War* is vain;
Columbia's glory rests with you,
Our sails are full—sweet girls adieu.

Sung in the Deserter.

SOME how my spindle I mislaid,
  And lost it underneath the grass,
Damon advancing, bow'd his head,
  And said, What seek you, pretty lass?
A little love, but urg'd with care,
Oft leads a heart, and leads it far.

'Twas passing by yon spreading oak
  That I my spindle lost just now.
His knife then kindly Damon took,
  And from the tree he cut a bough:
            A little love, &c.

Thus did the youth his time employ,
  While me he tenderly beheld;
He talk'd of love, I leap'd for joy,
  For ah! my heart did fondly yield.
            A little love, &c.

This World is a Stage.

THIS world is a stage, where all men engage,
  And each acts his part in the throng;
There is nought but confusion, mere folly, delusion,
  And the rest of it all is a song, &c.

The parson so grave, says your souls he will save,
  And shew you the right from the wrong,
By piously teaching, and long winding preaching,
  He sets off his flock with a song, &c.

The statesman he smiles, at the time he beguiles,
  And feeds you with promises long,
He squeezes your hand, and calls you his friend,
  While he means nothing else but a song, &c.

The Doctor he fills you with balsams and pills,
  And tells you that you will live long,
But believe me 'tis true, its the guineas in view,
  And the rest of it all is a song, &c.

The soldier he rattles of sieges and battles,
  And wonders he has been among,
His preferment and merit are both like his spirit,
  You may see they are all but a song, &c.

The ship-master cries, see the clouds how they rise,
  Look about my brave boys, it blows strong,
Come fill me some flip, and I'll warrant the ship,
  Will as sure reach her port as a song, &c.

The drover he'll prattle of heifers and cattle,
  And parcels he has been among,
All day he will fret until he can cheat,
  Then he sells off his stots with a song, &c.

The silly old prude, she will say you are rude,
　　If you touch but her hand in the throng,
But bring her aside, and you'll manage her pride,
　　And her virtue bring down to a song, &c.

The gentle coquette, she is all in a pett,
　　At morning if toy let be wrong,
All day she will pass consulting her glass,
　　And at night die away with a song, &c.

Come let us be merry, drive hence melancholy,
　　Since we are brave fellows among,
Let's each fill our glasses, taste life as it passes,
　　And each of us sing a good song, &c.

A favorite Scots Song.

WHEN lav'rocks sweet and yellow broom
　　Presume the banks of Tweed,
Blithe Nancy boasts a sweeter bloom,
　　Her charms all charms exceed.
Gang o'er the merry fields of hay,
Cry'd love-sick Jockey, wi' a sigh;
　　And wha sae saft, sae young and gay,
　　Cou'd sic a handsome lad deny?

In Sandy's cheek the white and red,
　　Like rose and lily join'd;
For him each lassie hung her head,
　　For her each ladie pin'd.
Gang o'er the merry field of hay,
　　Wi' me, my dearest lass, he'd cry;
And wha sae saft, sae young, and gay,
　　Cou'd sic a handsome lad deny?

He gang'd o'er fields and broomy land,
　　'Till mither 'gan to chide;
Then Sandy press'd her lily hand,
　　And ask'd her for his bride:
Then o'er the merry fields of hay,
　　Said she, my dearest lad, we'll hie;
For wha sae saft, sae young, and gay,
　　Cou'd sic a handsome lad deny?

When kind Friends, &c.

WHEN kind friends expect a song,
    Something new and striking:
Surely he can ne'er be wrong,
    Who gives each his liking.

Patriots like to get a place,
    The courtiers theirs to keep:
Country 'squires to drink and chase,
    And cits to eat and sleep.

Parsons like a bishopric,
    Gamblers like to bubble;
Doctors like to see friends sick,
    Lawyers theirs in trouble.

Soldiers like both peace and pay,
    When fighting is no more;
Sailors like a road to stray,
    For gold to wash ashore.

Ruddy bullies like to bluster,
    Pale beaux to seem polite;
Train-band Captains like a muster,
    But neither like to fight.

Ladies like—a thousand things,
    But yet it were not well;
He who for his pleasure sings,
    Should all their likings tell.

SONG.

COME now, all ye social pow'rs,
    Shed your influ'ence o'er us;
Crown with joy our present hours,
    Enliven those before us:
    Bring the flask, the music bring,
        Joy shall quickly find us;
    Sport and dance, and laugh and sing,
        And cast dull care behind us.

Love, thy god-head I adore,
    Source of gen'rous passion:

Nor will we ever bow before
  Those idols—Wealth or Fashion.
                Bring the flask, &c.

Why the plague shou'd we be sad,
  Whilst on earth we moulder;
Rich or poor, or grave or mad,
  We every day grow older.
                Bring the flask, &c.

Friendship! O thy smiles divine,
  Bright in all thy features;
What but friendship, love, and wine,
  Can make us happy creatures.
                Bring the flask, &c.

Since the time will steal away,
  Spite of all our sorrow,
Let's be blithe and gay to-day,
  And never mind to-morrow.

    Bring the flask, the music bring,
      Joy shall quickly find us:
    Sport and dance, and laugh and sing,
      And cast dull care behind us.

═══════

Get married as fast as you can.

YE virgins attend, believe me your friend,
  And with prudence adhere to my plan,
Ne'er let it be said, there goes an old maid,
  But get marry'd as fast as you can.

As soon as you find your hearts are inclin'd
  To beat quick at the sight of a man;
Then chuse out a youth, with honor and truth,
  And get marry'd as fast as you can.

For age like a cloud your charms soon will shroud,
  And this whimsical life's but a span;
Then, maids, make your hay, while Sol darts his ray,
  And get marry'd as fast as you can.

The treacherous rake will artfully take
  Ev'ry method poor girls to trepan;
But baffle the snare, and make virtue your care,
  And get marry'd as fast as you can.

And, when Hymen's bands have join'd both your
　　hands,
　The bright flame ſtill continue to fan ;
Ne'er harbour the ſtings that jealouſy brings,
　But be conſtant and bleſt while you can.

SONG.

MY days have been ſo wondrous free,
　　The little birds that fly
With careleſs eaſe from tree to tree,
　Were but as bleſs'd as I.

Aſk gliding waters, if a tear
　Of mine increaſ'd their ſtream ?
Or aſk the flying gales, if e'er
　I lent a ſigh to them ?
But now my former days retire,
　And I'm by beauty caught ;
The tender chains of ſweet deſire
　Are fix'd upon my thought.

An eager hope within my breaſt
　Does every doubt controul ;
And lovely Nancy ſtands confeſt
　The fav'rite of my ſoul.

Ye nightingales, ye twiſting pines,
　Ye ſwains that haunt the grove,
Ye gentle echoes, breezy winds !
　Ye cloſe retreats of love !

With all of nature, all of art,
　Aſſiſt the dear deſign ;
O teach a young unpractiſ'd heart
　To make her ever mine.

The very thought of change I hate,
　As much as of deſpair ;
Nor ever covet to be great,
　Unleſs it be for her.

'Tis true, the paſſion in my mind
　Is mix'd with ſoft diſtreſs ;
Yet while the fair I love is kind,
　I cannot wiſh it leſs.

The Virgin unmasked.

IT is I believe,
  Next Hollantide eve,
A twelvemonth since first I began
  To hold up my head,
  In love to be read,
And to construe the looks of a man,
And to construe the looks of a man.
  Young Damon I saw,
  He kiss'd me, Oh la!
I vow through my bosom it ran;
  My lips he so press'd,
  'Tis true I protest,
I thought him a duce of a man.
  Philander the gay
  I met at the play,
My heart beat a furious ratan;
  Because you must know,
  I some time ago,
Had hopes of his being the man.
  Brisk Strephon came next,
  But then I was vex'd,
He play'd with Miss Phillis's fan;
  I own, to be sure,
  I could not endure
To see myself robb'd of a man.
  My mother and aunts,
  Still watching my haunts,
Obstruct me as much as they can,
  But what do I care,
  I vow and declare,
I'll fit myself soon with a man.

The Stag through the Forest.

THE stag thro' the forest, when rouz'd by the horn,
  Sore frighted, high bounding, flies wretched, forlorn,
Quick panting, heart bursting, the hounds now in view,
Speed doubles! speed doubles! they eager pursue:
But escaping the hunters, again thro' the groves,
Forgetting past evils, with freedom he roves;
Not so in his soul who from tyrant love flies;
The shaft overtakes him, despairing he dies.

The Cobler.

A COBLER there was, and he liv'd in a stall,
Which serv'd him for parlour, for kitchen, and hall,
No coin in his pocket, nor care in his pate,
No ambition had he, nor duns at his gate:
  Derry down, down, down, derry down.

Contented he work'd, and he thought himself happy,
If at night he could purchase a jug of brown nappy:
How he'd laugh then, and whistle, and sing too most sweet!
Saying, just to a hair I have made both ends to meet:
  Derry down, down, &c.

But love, the disturber of high and of low,
That shoots at the peasant as well as the beau;
He shot the poor cobler quite through the heart,
I wish he had hit some more ignoble part:
  Derry down, down, &c.

It was from a cellar this archer play,
Where a buxom young damsel continually lay;
Her eyes shone so bright when she rose ev'ry day,
That she shot the poor cobler quite over the way:
  Derry down, down, &c.

He sung her love songs as he sat at his work,
But she was as hard as a Jew or a Turk;
Whenever he spake, she would flounce and would fleer,
Which put the poor cobler quite into despair;
  Derry down, down, &c.

He took up his awl that he had in the world,
And to make away with himself was resolv'd;
He pierc'd through his body instead of his sole,
So the cobler he died, and the bell it did toll.
  Derry down, down, &c.

And now, in good will, I advise as a friend,
All coblers take warning by this cobler's end:
Keep your hearts out of love, for we find by what's past,
That love brings us all to an end at the last.
  Derry down, down, &c.

Friend and Pitcher.

THE wealthy fool, with gold in store,
　Will still desire to grow richer,
Give me but health, I ask no more,
　My charming girl, my friend and pitcher.

My friend so rare, my girl so fair,
　With such, what mortal can be richer;
Give me but these, a fig for care,
　With my sweet girl, my friend and pitcher.

From morning sun I'd never grieve,
　To toil a hedger or a ditcher,
If that, when I came home at eve,
　I might enjoy my friend and pitcher.
　　My friend so rare, &c.

Tho' fortune ever shuns my door,
　I know not what can thus bewitch her;
With all my heart can I be poor,
　With my sweet girl, my friend and pitcher.
　　My friend so rare, &c.

The Taylor done over.

A TAYLOR I once was as blithe as e'er need be,
　Until love's alarms has a devil sure made me;
I that one was so lusty, and call'd Will the Rover,
Am now a poor skeleton. Oh, I'm done over.
　　Over, over, &c.

How many a day have I stood with great pleasure
And cut out my cloth to my customer's measure;
With a full yard of cabbage I then liv'd in clover,
But now I'm a skeleton, by Cupid done over.
　　Over, over, &c.

When first I beheld her in silks dress'd so gaily,
I fell into fits, and they trouble me daily;
Oh! how cruel must she be? the sight could not
　　move her,
I fear that these fits will soon do me over.
　　Over, over, &c.

The next time I saw her pass by my shop window,
My goose (being hot) burnt a sleeve to a cinder,

he girls do so jeer me, that I can go no where,
Was ever a poor taylor so fairly done over?
     Over, over, &c.

The last time I saw her was with a bold sailor,
She pointed and said—There's a done over taylor;
Good bye, Mr. Stitchlouse, I'm going to Dover,
The stroke was so great, it has quite done me over.
     Over, over, &c.

So now she has left me, and is gone with a sailor,
She has left me alone, a poor done over taylor!
I ne'er more will cabbage, nor be Will the Rover,
God send I was dead, for I'm fairly done over.
     Over, over, &c.

Retirement.

I ENVY not the proud their wealth,
 Their equipage and state:
Give me but innocence and health,
 I ask not to be great.

I in this sweet retirement find
 A joy unknown to kings,
For sceptres to a virtuous mind
 Seem vain and empty things.

Great Cincinnatus at his plough
 With brighter lustre shone,
Than guilty Cæsar e'er could shew,
 Though seated on a throne.

Tumultuous days, and restless nights,
 Ambition ever knows,
A stranger to the calm delights
 Of study and repose.

Then free from envy, care, and strife,
 Keep me, ye powers divine!
And pleas'd, when ye demand my life,
 May I that life resign!

A New Negro Song.
Tune——BOBIN JOAN.

ME be one poor slave, brought into Barbado,
  Ven one pickaninny, such de cruel trado,
How me vetch and carry, now go here and dere,
Dey no let me rest, dey for black man no care, sir.
            Tol de rol, de rol.

Now chain'd like de horse, and de weder hot,
Vipt along de road, poor negro go to pot;
If me faint or dying, still along must go;
Devil take de driver, him always serve me so.
            Tol de rol, &c.

If me stay at home, still me run about, sir,
Now up, now down, now kick, now vip, now in and out, sir;
My massa swear, my missa scold, if I no come de faser,
I could not be used vorse, if old Nick he was my massa.
            Tol de rol, &c.

De pickaninnies too, de littel boy and miss, sir,
Dey laugh and call me name, and tump me wit dere fis, sir;
Yet me must not complain, poor negro must endure
Alas! a well-a-day, dere be no means to cure it.
            Tol de rol, &c.

All de night and day, me be toiling, moiling,
Never can be rest, but ever sweat and broiling;
Me, poor negro, black, all dat's hard be trying,
White man use me so, me wish dat I vas dying.
            Tol de rol, &c.

SONG.

NO glory I covet, no riches I want,
  Ambition is nothing to me;
The one thing I beg of kind heaven to grant,
  Is a mind, independent and free.

With passions unruffled, untainted with pride,
  By reason my life let me square;
The wants of my nature are cheaply supply'd,
  And the rest are but folly and care.

The blessings which Providence freely has lent,
   I'll justly and gratefully prize;
Whilst sweet meditation and cheerful content
   Shall make me both healthy and wise.

In the pleasures the great man's possessions display,
   Unenvy'd, I'll challenge my part;
For every fair object my eyes can survey,
   Contributes to gladden my heart.

How vainly, through infinite trouble and strife,
   The many their labors employ!
Since all, that is truly delightful in life,
   Is what all, if they please, may enjoy.

Leave off your foolish Prating.

LEAVE off your foolish prating,
   Talk no more of Whig and Tory,
But drink your glass, round let it pass,
   The bottle stanks before ye.

CHORUS.

   Fill it up to the top,
Let the night with mirth be crown'd;
   Drink about, see it out,
Love and friendship still go round.

If claret be a blessing,
   This night devote to pleasure:
Let wordly cares, and state affairs,
   Be thought on at more leisure.

Chorus—Fill it up to the top, &c.

If any is so zealous
   To be a party minion,
Let him drink like me, we'll soon agree,
   And be of one opinion.

CHORUS.

   Fill your glass, name your lass,
See her health go swiftly round;
   Drink about, see it out,
Let the night with mirth be crown'd.

Jockey to the Fair.

'TWAS on the morn of sweet May day,
    When nature painted all things gay,
Taught birds to sing, and lambs to play,
    And gild the meadows rare :
Young Jockey, early in the dawn,
Arose, and tript it o'er the lawn ;
His Sunday's coat the youth put on,
For Jenny had vow'd away to run
    With Jockey to the fair.

Jenny had vow'd, &c.

The chearful parish bells had rung,
With eager steps he trudg'd along,
With flow'ry garlands round him hung,
    Which shepherds us'd to wear :
He tapt the window—Haste my dear,
Jenny, impatient, cry'd—Who's there ?
'Tis I, my love, and no one near ;
Step gently down, you've nought to fear
    With Jockey to the fair.

My dad and mam are fast asleep,
My brother's up, and with the sheep ;
And will you still your promise keep,
    Which I have heard you swear ?
And will you ever constant prove ?
I will, by all the powers of love,
And ne'er deceive my charming dove ;
Dispel these doubts, and haste, my love,
    With Jockey to the fair.

Behold the ring, the shepherd cry'd,
Will Jenny be my charming bride ?
Let Cupid be our happy guide,
    And hymen meet us there.
Then Jockey did his vows renew,
He wou'd be constant, would be true :
His word was pledg'd—away she flew
With cowslips, tipt with balmy dew,
    With Jockey to the fair.

In raptures meet the joyful throng,
Their gay companions blith and young ;
Each join the dance, each join the song,
    And hail the happy pair.

In turns there's none so fond as they,
They bless'd the kind propitious day,
The smiling morn of blooming May,
When lovely Jenny run away
  With Jockey to the fair.

'Tis Wine that clears, &c.

'TIS wine that clears the understanding,
  Makes men learned without books;
It fits the general for commanding,
  And gives soldiers fiercer looks.

'Tis wine that gives a life to lovers,
  Heightens beauties of the fair:
Truth from falsehood it discovers,
  Quickens joys, and conquers care,
Wine will set our souls on fire,
  Fit us for all glorious things;
When rais'd by Bacchus, we aspire,
  At flights above the reach of kings.

Bring in *bonum magnums* plenty,
  Be each glass a bumper crown'd;
None to flinch, till they be empty,
  And full fifty toasts gone round.

The Tempest of War.

LET the tempest of war
  Be heard from afar,
With trumpets' and cannons' alarms:
  Let the brave, if they will,
  By their valour and skill,
Seek honor and conquest in arms.

  To live safe, and retire,
  Is what I desire,
Of my flocks and my Chloe possest;
  For in them I obtain
  True peace without pain,
And the lasting enjoyment of rest.

  In some cottage or cell,
  Like a shepherd to dwell,

From all interruption at ease;
　In a peaceable life,
　To be blest with a wife,
Who will study her husband to please.

Drunk I was last Night.

DRUNK I was last night, that's poz,
　My wife began to scold;
Say what I cou'd for my heart's blood,
　Her clack she would not hold.

Thus her chat she did begin,
　Is this your time of coming in?
The clock strikes one, you'll be undone,
　If thus you lead your life.

My dear, said I, I can't deny,
　But what you say is true;
I do intend my life to mend,
　Pray lend's the pot to spew.

Fy, you sot, I ne'er can bear
　To rise thus ev'ry night;
Though, like a beast, you never care
　What consequence comes by't.

The child and I may starve for you;
　We neither can have half our due;
With grief I find, you're so unkind,
　In time you'll break my heart.

At that I smil'd, and said, dear child,
　I believe your in the wrong;
But if't should be your destiny,
　I'll sing a merry song.

The Storm.

CEASE, rude Boreas, blust'ring railer!
　List, ye landsmen, all to me!
Messmates, hear a brother sailor
　Sing the dangers of the sea;
From bounding billows, first in motion,
　When the distant whirlwinds rise,
To the tempest troubled ocean,
　Where the seas contend with skies!

Hark! the boatswain hoarsely bawling,
  By topsail sheets, and haulyards stand!
Down top-gallants quick be hauling,
  Down your stay-sails, hand, boys, hand!
Now it freshens, set the braces,
  The topsail sheets now let go!
Luff boys, luff! don't make wry faces,
  Up your topsails nimbly clew.

Now all you on down beds sporting,
  Fondly lock'd in beauty's arms;
Fresh enjoyments, wanton courting,
  Safe from all but love's alarms;
Round us roars the tempest louder;
  Think what fears our minds enthrall;
Harder yet, it yet blows harder,
  Now again the boatswain calls!

The topsail yards point to the wind, boys,
  See all clear to reef each course;
Let the fore sheet go, don't mind, boys,
  Though the weather should be worse.
Fore and aft the sprit-sail yard get,
  Reef the mizen, see all clear
Hands up, each preventure brace set,
  Man the fore-yard, cheer, lads, cheer!

Now the dreadful thunder's roaring,
  Peal on peal contending clash,
On our heads fierce rain falls pouring.
  In our eyes blue lightnings flash.
One wide water all around us,
  All above us one black sky;
Different deaths at once surround us,
  Hark! what means that dreadful cry?

The foremast's gone, cries every tongue out,
  O'er the lee, twelve feet 'bove deck;
A leak beneath the chest tree's sprung out,
  Call all hands to clear the wreck.
Quick the lanyards cut to pieces,
  Come, my hearts, be stout and bold;
Plumb the well—the leak increases,
  Four feet water in the hold,

While o'er the ſhip wild waves are beating,
   We for wives or children mourn ;
Alas ! from hence there's no retreating,
   Alas ! to them there's no return.
Still the leak is gaining on us ;
   Both chain pumps are choak'd below.
Heav'n have mercy here upon us !
   For only that can ſave us now.

O'er the lee-beam is the land, boys,
   Let the guns o'erboard be thrown :
To the pump come ev'ry hand, boys,
   See ! our mizen-maſt is gone.
The leak we've found it cannot pour faſt,
   We've lighten'd her a foot or more ;
Up, and rig a jury fore-maſt,
   She rights, ſhe rights, boys, we're off ſhore.

Now once more on joys we're thinking,
   Since kind Heav'n has ſav'd our lives ;
Come, the can, boys ! let's be drinking
   To our ſweethearts and our wives,
Fill it up, about ſhip wheel it,
   Cloſe to our lips a brimmer join,
Where's the tempeſt now, who feels it ?
   None—the dangers drown'd in wine.

Bonny Bet.

NO more I'll court the town-bred fair,
   Who ſhines in artificial beauty ;
For native charms, without compare,
   Claim all my love, reſpect and duty.

CHORUS.

O my bonny, bonny Bet, ſweet bloſſom,
   Was I a king, ſo proud to wear thee,
From off the verdant couch I'd bear thee,
To grace thy faithful lover's boſom.
         O my bonny, bonny Bet, &c.

Yet aſk me where thoſe beauties lie,
   I cannot ſay in ſmile or dimple ;
In blooming cheeks, or radiant eye—
   'Tis happy nature, wild and ſimple.
         O my bonny, bonny Bet, &c.

Let dainty beaux for ladies pine,
   And sigh in numbers trite and common;
Ye gods! one darling wish to mine,
   And all I ask is lovely woman.
                O my bonny, bonny Bet.

Come, dearest girl, the rosy bowl,
   Like thy bright eye, with pleasure dancing;
My heav'n art thou, so take my soul,
   With rapture ev'ry sense entrancing.
                O my bonny, bonny Bet.

When War's Alarms.

WHEN war's alarms entic'd my Willy from me,
   My poor heart with grief did sigh;
Each fond remembrance brought fresh sorrow on me,
   'Woke ere yet the morn was nigh:
     No other could delight him;
     Ah! Why did I e'er flight him,
Coldly answ'ring his fond tale,
Which drove him far amid the rage of war,
   And left silly me thus to bewail.

But I no longer, tho' a maid forsaken,
   Thus will mourn like yonder dove,
For ere the lark to-morrow shall awaken,
   I will seek my absent love:
     The hostile country over
     I'll fly to seek my lover,
Scorning ev'ry threat'ning fear;
     Nor distant shore,
     Nor cannons roar,
Shall longer keep me from my dear.

Venus of Totterdown-Hill.

AT *Totterdown-hill* there dwelt an old pair,
   And it may be they dwell there still,
Much riches indeed didn't fall to their share,
   They kept a small farm and a mill:
But fully content with what they did get,
   They knew not of guile or of arts;

One daughter they had, and her name it was Bet,
  And she was the pride of their hearts.

Nut-brown were her locks, her shape it was straight,
  Her eyes were as black as a sloe :
Her teeth were milk-white, full smart was her gait,
  And sleek was her skin as a doe :
All thick were the clouds, and the rain it did pour,
  No bit of true blue could be spy'd,
A child wet and cold came and knock'd at the door,
  Its mam it had lost, and it cry'd.

Young Bet was as mild as the morning of May,
  The babe she hug'd close to her breast;
She chaf'd him all o'er, and smil'd as he lay,
  She kiss'd him, and lull'd him to rest:
But who do you think she had got for her prize?
  Why love the sly master of arts;
No sooner he wak'd, but he drop'd his disguise,
  And shew'd her his wings and his darts.

Quoth he, I am Love; but, oh, be not afraid,
  Tho' all I make shake at my will;
So good and kind have you been, my fair maid,
  No harm shall you feel from my skill;
My mother ne'er dealt with such fondness by me,
  A friend you shall find in me still;
Take my quiver and shoot, be greater than she,
  The *Venus* of *Totterdown-hill.*

The Sailor's Advice.

As you mean to set sail for the land of delight,
  And in wedlock's soft hammocks to swing ev'ry night,
If you hope that your voyage successful should prove,
Fill your sails with affection, your cabin with love.
        Fill your sails, &c.

Let your hearts like the main-mast, be ever upright,
And the union you boast, like our tackle be tight;
Of the shoals of Indiff'rence be sure to keep clear,
And the quicksands of jealousy never come near.
        And the quicksands, &c.

If husband's e'er hope to live peaceable lives,
They must reckon themselves, give the helm to their
    wives.
For the evener we go, boys, the better we sail,
And on ship-board the helm is still rul'd by the tail.
            And on ship-board, &c.

Then list to your pilot, my boy, and be wise;
If my precepts you scorn, and my maxims despise,
A brace of proud antlers your brows may adorn,
And a hundred to one but you double Cape Horn.
            And a hundred, &c.

Guardian Angel.

GUARDIAN angel now protect me,
    Send me to the swain I love;
Cupid with thy bow direct me,
    Help me, all ye powers above.
Bear him my sighs, ye gentle breezes,
    Tell him, I love and I despair;
        Tell him, for him I grieve,
        Say 'tis for him I live;
    O may the shepherd be sincere!

Thro' the shadowy groves I'll wander,
    Silent as the bird of night:
Near the brink of yonder fountain,
    First Leander bless'd my sight,
Witness, ye groves and falls of water,
    Echoes, repeat the vows he swore:
        Can he forget me,
        Will he neglect me,
    Shall I never see him more!

Does he love and yet forsake me,
    To admire a nymph more fair?
If 'tis so, I'll wear the willow,
    And esteem the happy pair.
Some lonely cave I'll make my dwelling,
    Ne'er more the cares of life pursue:
        The lark and philomel,
        Only shall hear me tell,
    What makes me bid the world adieu.

The Echoing Horn.

THE echoing horn calls the sportsmen abroad,
　　To horse, my brave boys, and away;
The morning is up, and the cry of the hounds
　　Upbraids our too tedious delay.

What pleasure we find in pursuing the fox!
　　O'er hill and o'er valley he flies;
Then follow, we'll soon overtake him—huzza!
　　The traitor is seiz'd on and dies.

Triumphant, returning at night with the spoil,
　　Like Bacchanals, shouting and gay,
How sweet with the bottle and lass to refresh,
　　And lose the fatigues of the day!

With sport, love and wine, fickle fortune defy:
　　Dull wisdom all happiness fours:
Since life is no more than a passage at best,
　　Let's strew the way over with flow'rs.

The Banks of Kentucke.
Tune—Banks of the Dee.

THE spring was advancing, and birds were beginning
　　To sing on the boughs of each purling brook;
On the early green herbage at leisure reclining,
　　I was carelessly viewing the banks of Kentucke.
Hail stranger to song! hail deep-channel'd river,
　　Thy prominent cliffs shall be famous forever;
Thy high-swelling floods henceforward shall never
　　Obscurely roll down thro' the banks of Kentucke.

Disgusted with idle, romantic pretensions,
　　The populous city I lonely forsook;
Delighted in nature with fond apprehensions,
　　I eagerly came to the banks of Kentucke.
O, never did art so much beauty discover,
　　To reward the long search of its most raptur'd lover,
As nature's luxuriant fancy spreads over
　　The gay fertile soil on the banks of Kentucke.

Her genius shall rove with an endless desire,
  Improvements to make without learning or book:
While virtue and truth shall forever conspire,
  To bless those that dwell on the banks of Kentucke.
Here, far from tyrannical power remov'd,
  The spirit of freedom shall haply be prov'd;
The patriot shall by his country be lov'd,
  And live without guile on the banks of Kentucke.

Here bigotry never shall raise its foul banner.
  The basis of joy thro' all ages it shook;
The young and the aged in more happy manner
  Than those shall improve on the banks of Kentucke.
In honest industry their time still employing,
  With heart-cheering mirth all their meetings enjoying.
With the blessings of friendship, and love never cloying,
  All ranks shall unite on the banks of Kentucke.

Rich plenty and health, with visage all glowing,
  Invite and allure us with promising look;
Never more to regret other rivers long flowing,
  Not such as glide down thro' the banks of Kentucke.
Pale sickness doth pass thro' the land as a stranger,
  No dreadful distemper here frightens the ranger,
As he passes thro' canebrakes and waters no danger
  Expecting to meet on the banks of Kentucke.

―――――

O the Days when I was Young.

O THE days when I was young,
  When I laugh'd in fortune's spite.
Talk'd of love the whole day long,
  And with nectar crown'd the night;
Then it was, old father Care,
  Little reck'd I of thy frown,
Half thy malice youth could bear,
  And the rest a bumper drown.
                    O the days, &c.

Truth, they say, lies in a well,
  Why, I vow, I ne'er could see;
Let the water drinkers tell—
  There it always lay for me :
For when sparkling wine went round,
  Never saw I falshood's mask :
But still the honest truth I found
  In the bottom of each flask.
              O the days, &c.

True, at length my vigour's flown,
  I have years to bring decay ;
Few the locks that now I own,
  And the few I have are grey ;
Yet, old Jerome, thou may boast,
  While thy spirits do not tire ;
Still beneath thy age's frost
  Glows a spark of youthful fire.
              O the days, &c.

New Tally Ho.

THE hunters are up and the ruddy fac'd morn,
  Most cheerful salute with the musical horn ;
The blue misty mountains seem join'd with the skies,
And the dogs yelp aloud as away Reynard flies:
Tally ho, tally ho, see the game is in view,
The sportsmen all cry as they nimbly pursue.

The high mettled steed sweeps away at the sound,
And the hills seem to move as they fly o'er the ground;
Each prospect is charming, all nature is gay,
And promises sport and success thro' the day,
Tally ho, tally ho, see the game is in view,
The sportsmen all cry as they nimbly pursue.

The goddess of pleasure, sweet rosy cheek'd health,
Gives joys more abundant than titles or wealth ;
And appetite gives to their viands a zest,
Above all the sauces by cooks ever drest.
Tally ho, tally ho, see the game is in view,
The sportsmen all cry as they nimbly pursue.

Huzza ! then my boys, to the chace let's away,
Nor indolence lose the delights of the day ;

From fashion and folly we borrow no grace,
But joy paints the cheeks as we follow the chace,
Tally ho, tally ho, see the game is in view,
The sportsmen all cry as they nimbly pursue.

Jacky Bull from France.

IN Jacky Bull, when bound for France,
    The gosling you discover;
But taught to ride, to fence and dance,
    A finish'd goose comes over.
With his tierce and carte—fa! fa!
And his cotillion so smart—ha! ha!
He charms each female heart—oh, la!
    As Jacky returns from Dover.

For cocks and dogs, see 'squire at home,
    The prince of country tonies;
Return'd from Paris, Spa, or Rome,
    Our 'squire's a nice Adonis.
With his tierce and carte—fa! fa!
And his cotillion so smart—ha! ha!
He charms the female heart—oh, la!
    The pink of macaronies.

A New Sea Song.

WHEN gentle Zephyr fans the ocean,
    The playful waves in dimples gay,
Our cumb'rous bark scarce put in motion,
    We sailors make it holiday;
      In joyous ring,
      We sit and sing,
Of heroes fam'd with laurels crown'd;
      Old Benbow's fate,
      The crew relate,
In chorus, while the can goes round.

But when from northern regions bursting,
    Wild Boreas rushes o'er the deep,
For pleasures we no more are thirsting,
    But to our quarters instant leap:

　　　　Tho' billows roar,
　　　　Aloft we foar,
For failors hearts are never fcar'd;
　　　　While blows the gale,
　　　　We furl the fail,
Sufpended from the bending yard.

The watch revolving nightly keeping,
　The land defcry'd, of rocks aware,
Frefh pleafures from our dangers reaping,
　When moor'd in harbour with the fair;
　　　　In joyous ring,
　　　　We fit and fing,
Of heroes fam'd, with laurels crown'd;
　　　　Old Benbow's fate,
　　　　The crew relate,
In chorus, while the can goes round.

Amo Amas.

Amo amas,
　　I love a lafs,
As a cedar tall and flender:
　　Sweet cowflip's grace
　　Is her nom'tive cate,
And fhe's of the feminine gender.

CHORUS.

　　Rorum corum,
　　Sunt divorum,
　　Harum fcarum!
　　　Divo!—
Tag rag merry derry, perriwig and hat-band,
　Hic, hoc, horum, genitivo!
　　Can I decline
　　　A nymph divine?
　　Her voice as a flute is *dulcis;*
　　　Her *oculis* bright,
　　　Her *manus* white,
And foft, when I *tacto,* her pulfe is.
　　　　　Rorum, corum, &c.

Oh, how *bella*
My *puella!*
I'll kiss, *secula seculorum:*
If I've luck, Sir,
She's my *uxor;*
O *dies Benedictorum!*

Rorum, corum, &c.

When the Blythe Village-Maid, &c.

WHEN the blythe village-made leads her flocks
 to the plains,
 Ah, me! how I envy her lot!
I'd spurn at the splendor a palace contains,
 With freedom to dwell in a cot:
Awak'd by the lark, o'er my love as I hung,
 His slumbers I'd chace with a kiss;
No tyrant to check me, no venomous tongue,
 With slander to sully my bliss.
The toil of the day would be pleasure to me,
 Still drinking fresh health from the gale!
And ev'ning would bring, with an aspect of glee,
 The legend, the song, or the tale: |rest,
'Till the still gloom of night wrapp'd the hamlet in
 And my fancy grew big with alarms,
Then I'd steal to my lover, creep close to his breast,
 And lose all my fears in his arms.

A hunting Song.

THE sun from the east tips the mountains with
 gold,
And the mead was all spangled with drew-drops
 behold:
The larks early mattin proclaims the new day,
And the horn's cheerful summons rebukes our delay:
With the sports of the field there's no pleasures can
 vie,
While jocund we follow the hounds in full cry.

Let the drudge of the town make riches his sport,
And the slaves of the state hunt the smiles of the
 court:

No care nor ambition our patience annoy,
But innocence still gives a zest to our joy.
    With the sports of the field, &c.

Mankind are all hunters in various degrees;
The priest hunts a living, the lawyer his fees;
The doctor a patient, the courtier a place—
Tho' often, like us, they're flung out with disgrace.
    With the sports of the field, &c.

The cit hunts a plumb, the soldier hunts fame;
The poet a dinner, the patriot a name;
And the artful coquette, tho' she seems to refuse,
Yet, in spite of her airs, she her lover pursues.
    With the sports of the field, &c.

Let the bold and the busy hunt glory and wealth—
All the blessing we ask, is the blessing of health:
With hounds and with horns, thro' the woodlands
    we roam,
And when tir'd abroad, find contentment at home.
With the sports of the field there's no pleasures can
    vie,
While jocund we follow the hounds in full cry.

Farmer Dobbin's Complaint.

THREE daughters I have, and as prettily made,
 As handsome as any you'll see;
And lovers they count—but still I'm afraid
 They always will hang upon me.

In writing of letters and talking of love,
 They are foolishly spending their time;
One gives them a ribbon, and one a new glove;
 And thus they are passing their prime.

These bucks of the town—with their elegant coats,
 I'm sick of their horses and chairs;
They plunder my hay, and they pilfer my oats—
 Am I keeping a tavern my dears?

This courting and courting, and never concluding,
 Is nonsense—(I'm sorry to say)
Your kissing and playing is rather intruding,
 Unless you will—take them away.

How imperfect is Expression.

HOW imperfect is expression,
   Some emotions to impart,
When we mean a soft confession,
   And yet seek to hide the heart!
When our bosoms, all complying,
   With delicious tumults swell,
And beat, what broken, faltring, dying,
   Language would, but cannot tell!

Deep confusion's rosy terror,
   Quite expressive, paints my cheek:
Ask no more—behold your error—
   Blushes eloquently speak.
What, tho' silent is my anguish,
   Or breath'd only to the air,
Mark my eyes, and as they languish,
   Read what your's have written there.

O that you could once conceive me!
   Once my soul's strong feeling view!
Love has nought more fond, believe me;
   Friendship nothing half so true.
From you, I am wild, despairing;
   With you, speechless as I touch!
This is all that bears declaring,
   And, perhaps, declares too much.

A Lover's Farewell.

HARK, dear girl, the message hear,
   The call I must obey,
And tho' mine eyes drop many a tear,
   Yet, yet I must not stay;
Farewell my life, my friend adieu,
I leave my heart in leaving you.

The compass guides the mariner
   Who sails from pole to pole,
Attraction helps the comet far
   Her pond'rous orb to roll,
But thou'rt my magnet when I roam
To attract me to my native home.

Tho' I must try the tossing main,
  And seek a distant port,
Yet if you'r kind its rage is vain,
  Should I be Fortune's sport:
Now all I ask the gods to do,
Is that they'll make me worthy you,
But if I'm doom'd by fate to find
  Your heart is not for me,
Ye wat'ry powers! prove more kind,
  And wreck me in your sea—
Thus, thus I'll bid a long adieu
To love, to happiness, and you.

The Maid of the Mill.

WILLIAM.

I'VE kiss and I've prattled with fifty fair maids,
  And chang'd them as oft do ye see;
But of all the fair maidens that dance on the green
  The maid of the mill for me.

PHOEBE.

There's fifty young men have told me fine tales,
  And call'd me the fairest she;
But of all the gay youths that sport on the green,
  Young Harry's the lad for me.

WILLIAM.

Her eyes are as black as the sloe in the hedge,
  Her face like the blossoms in May,
Her teeth are as white as the new shorn flock,
  Her breath like the new made hay.

PHOEBE.

He's tall and he's straight as the poplar tree,
  His cheeks are as fresh as a rose;
He looks like a squire of high degree
  When drest in his Sunday's clothes.

The general Hunt.

TO horse, ye jolly sportsmen,
  And greet the new-born day:

Inceſſant, lo! thro' Nature's field,
   Each creature hunts his prey.
              And a-hunting, &c.

Dame Nature teaches Reynard craft
   To o'er-reach the feather'd flocks;
And we purſue the chiding dogs,
   While they run down the fox.

Mankind hunt one another;
   Your great men hunt the ſmall;
Some hunt for heav'n, and ſome for hell;
   Old Satan hunts us all.

Some fain would hunt for honour,
   A game that's hard to find;
The needy hunt for charity,
   And may go hunt the wind.

Our patriots loudly bellow,
   The nation's deſp'rate caſe,
While all their ſtir and buſtle's made
   In hunting out a place.

Full cry the tories hunt the whigs,
   Who in their turn purſue;
And running one another down,
   Run down their country too.

The lawyer hunts out quibbles,
   Your title to maintain;
He'll hunt the right 'till it be wrong,
   Then hunt it back again.

The toper daily hunts his pot,
   Both care and ſenſe to drown;
Whilſt gameſters hunt another's purſe,
   And loſe ſight of their own.

The laſſes hunt their lovers,
   Each lover hunts his laſs:
The fop, in chace of his dear face,
   Hunts out his looking-glaſs.

O'er hill and dale, with hound and horn,
   Lets hunt, boys, while 'tis light;

Then joyous we'll o'er flowing bowls
  Revive the chase at night.
                    And a-hunting, &c.

Good-morrow to your Night-cap.

DEAR Kathleen, you, no doubt,
  Find sleep how very sweet 'tis;
Dogs bark, and cocks have crowed out;
  You never dream how late 'tis.
    This morning gay
    I post away,
To have with you a bit of play:
    On two legs rid
    Along to bid
Good-morrow to your night-cap.

Last night a little bowsy
  With wisky, ale and cyder,
I ask'd young Betty Blowzy
  To let me sit beside her:
    Her anger rose,
    And sour as sloes,
The little jipsy cock'd her nose:
    Yet here I've rid
    Along to bid
Good morrow to your night cap.

Beneath the honey-suckle,
  The daisy and the violet
Compose so sweet a truckle,
  They'll tempt you sure to spoil it.
    Sweet Sal and Bell
    I've pleas'd so well—
But hold, I must'nt kiss and tell;
    So here I've rid
    Along to bid
Good-morrow to your night-cap.

No, Indeed, not I.

ONE summer's eve, when Luna's beam
  Illumin'd hill and dale,

And gaily wanton'd on the ſtream,
  With zephyr's gentle gale;
What, all alone, my pretty maid,
  Cry'd Colin, paſſing by,
Take company—I flouting ſaid,
  Indeed, ſir, no not I.

O let me, ſaid the ſmiling ſwain,
  Conduct you through the grove;
And then, in fond and moving ſtrain,
  Renew'd his tale of love.
He begg'd I'd name the happy day,
  And hop'd the ſame was nigh;
Says I, ha' done—I cannot ſtay—
  Indeed, ſays he—nor I.

We parted; but the teſty youth,
  In female arts untaught,
Miſtook my meaning, for in truth
  I meant not as he thought.
Then threw me oft' in Colin's way,
  And ſmil'd when he came nigh;
Again he wou'd, cou'd I ſay nay—
  Why, no, indeed, not I.

I am not Twenty.

AS through the grove, the other day,
  I gang'd ſo blithe and bonny;
Who ſhould I meet upon the way,
  But my own true love Johnny!
    With eager haſte,
    He claſp'd my waiſt,
And kiſſes gave me plenty;
    Tho, I deny'd,
    And thus reply'd,
" Dear lad—I am not twenty."

What's that to me, the ſhepherd cry'd,
  You're old enough to marry;
Then come, dear laſs, and be my bride,
  No longer let us tarry:

But let's be gone,
　　　　O'er yonder lawn,
　　Where lads and lasses plenty,
　　　Are fill'd with joy,
　　　And kiss and toy,
Altho' they are not twenty.

I listen'd to his soothing tale,
　And gang'd wi' him so rarely;
With song and pipe he did prevail,
　He won my wishes fairly:
　　　O he's the lad,
　　　That makes me glad,
　　With kisses sweet and plenty;
　　　So I declare,
　　　By all that's fair,
I'll wed—tho' not quite twenty.

―――――

The Linnet.

AS passing by a shady grove,
　　I heard a linnet sing,
Whose sweetly plaintive voice of love,
　Proclaim'd the chearful spring.
His pretty accents seem'd to flow,
　As if he knew no pain,
His downy throat he tun'd so sweet,
　It echo'd o'er the plain.

Ah! happy warbler (I reply'd)
　Contented thus to be;
'Tis only harmony and love,
　Can be compar'd to thee.
Thus perch'd upon the spray you stand,
　The monarch of the shade;
And even sip ambrosial sweets,
　That glow from ev'ry glade.

Did man possess but half thy bliss,
　How joyful might he be!
But man was never form'd for this,
　'Tis only joy for thee.

Then farewell, pretty bird (I said)
  Pursue thy plantive tale,
And let thy tuneful accents spread
  All o'er the fragrant vale.

My Love is gone to Sea.

MY love is gone to sea,
  Whilst I his absence mourn,
No joy shall smile on me,
Until my love return.
He ask'd me for his bride,
And many vows he swore;
I blush'd—and soon comply'd,
My heart was his before.

One little month was past,
And who so blest as we?
The summons came at last,
And Jemmy must to sea.
I saw his ship so gay
Swift fly the wave-worn shore;
I wip'd my tears away—
And saw his ship no more.

When clouds shut in the sky.
And storms around me howl;
When livid lightnings fly,
And threat'ning thunders roll;
All hopes of rest are lost,
No slumbers visit me,
My anxious thoughts are tost
With Jemmy on the sea.

The Dauphin.

YE sons of Mars, attend,
  Come join the festive throng,
In loftiest strains exult,
  For Jove approves the song.
Let gladness ev'ry heart expand,
  Let gratitude inspire

D 2

Each patriot's breast with joy unfeign'd
  To hail the royal Sire!
A Dauphin's born, let cannons loud
  Bid echo rend the sky;
Long life to Gallia's king,
  Columbia's great ally.

Hark, hark! a feu de joye—
  Makes trembling æther ring,
While shouting armies hail
  A prince, a future king;
On whom may heaven with liberal hand,
  Its choicest gifts bestow:
May peace and wisdom bless his reign,
  And lawrels grace his brow.
A Dauphin's born, &c.

  To visit earth once more,
Lo, lo! Austrea deigns;
  The golden age returns,
Now truth and justice reigns:
  See, proud oppression hides its head,
Fell tyranny expires,
  For independence, heaven's fair gift,
Lights freedom's sacred fires.
  A Dauphin's born, &c.

Hunting Song.

HARK! hark! the joy-inspiring horn
  Salutes the rosy rising morn,
And echoes through the dale;
With clam'rous peals the hills resound,
The hounds quick-scented scow'r the ground,
  And snuff the fragrant gale.

Nor gates nor hedges can impede
The brisk, high-mettled, starting steed,
  The jovial pack pursue;
Like light'ning darting o'er the plains,
The distant hills with speed he gains,
  And sees the game in view.

Her path the timid hare forsakes,
And to the copse for shelter makes,
  There pants a while for breath;
When now the noise alarms her ear,
Her haunts descry'd, her fate is near,
  She sees approaching death.

Directed by the well-known breeze,
The hounds their trembling victim seize,
  She faints, she falls, she dies:
The distant coarsers now come in,
And join the loud triumphant din,
  'Till echo rends the skies.

***

The Honey-Moon.

WOU'D you know, my good friends, what the honey-moon is,
How long in duration, how perfect in bliss.
A proof may be found, and a sample be seen,
In some boarding school couple just left Gretna green,
    My dearest, my duck,
    My sweetest, my chuck;
Miss Kitty's an Angel, her Billy a God;
    Whips crack, glasses jingle,
    While sighs intermingle,
And Cupid ascents, and goes niddity nod,
    Niddity nod, niddity nod,
O'er Kitty the Angel, and Billy the God.

Papa's and Mama's surly tempers once past,
Bright Bloomsbury-square has this couple at last!
In three weeks possession, how pleasures will cloy!
Neglect hurts the lady, and time cools the boy.
    So impatient to roam:—
    Ma'am you're never at home,
A path so vexatious no wife ever trod;
    My torment, my curse;—
    You are bad. You are worse.
While Cupid flies off, from a quarrel so odd,
    Niddity nod, niddity nod,
And Miss is no Angel, and Billy no God.

To routs hies the lady, to gambling goes master;
To part from each other ne'er couple went faster,
While raking at night, and distraction at noon,
Soon close all the joys of the sweet honey-moon.
    Bleeding hearts, aching heads,
      Sep'rate tables and beds,
Render wedlock's sweet countenance dull as a clod,
    Then hie for a summons
      From grave Doctors Commons,
While Proctors and parchments go niddity nod,
    Niddity nod, niddity nod,
O'er Kitty the Angel, and Billy the God.

Plato.

SAYS Plato why should man be vain?
   Since bounteous Heaven has made him great!
Why looketh he with insolent disdain
   On those undeck'd with wealth or state!
Can splended robes or beds of down,
   Or costly gems that deck the fair?
Can all the glories of a crown,
   Give health, or ease the brow of care?
The scepter'd king, the burthen'd slave,
   The humble and the haughty die:
The rich, the poor, the base, the brave,
   In dust without distinction lie.
Go, search the tombs were monarch's rest,
   Who once the greatest titles bore:
The wealth and glory they possest,
   And all their honours are no more.
So glides the meteor through the sky,
   And spreads along a guilded train:
But, when its short liv'd beauties die,
   Dissolves to common air again.
So 'tis with us, my jovial souls,
   Let friendship reign while here we stay,
Let's crown our joys with flowing bowls,
   When Jove commands we must away.

Edwin and Ella.

SEE beneath yon bow'r of roses,
   Sweetly sleeps the heav'nly maid;
'Tis my gentle love reposes,
   Softly tread the sacred shade.

Mark the loves that play around her,
   Mark my Ella's graceful mein;
See the wood-nymphs all surround her,
   Hailing Ella, beauty's queen.

Flutt'ring Cupids round decending,
   Soft expand their silken wings;
From the zephyr's breath defending,
   Ev'ry sweet that round her springs.

Sportive fancy, hear my prayer,
   Gently from thy airy throne,
Whisper to thy sleeping fair,
   Edwin lives for her alone.

SONG.*

SINCE love is the plan,
   I'll love if I can,
But first let me tell you what sort of a man:
In address how complete,
In dress spruce and neat,
No matter how tall so he's over five feet.
    Then this is my fancy,
    Such a man can I see,
    I'm his if he's mine,
      Until then I am free.

Tho' gentle he be,
His man he shall see,
Yet never be conquer'd by any but me;
In a dance bear a bob,
In a glass hob-a-nob,
Yet drink of reason his noddle ne'er rob.
    Then this is my fancy, &c.

  * Sung by Mrs. Morris in the Poor Soldier.

Happy, Harmless, Rural Pair.

HAPPY, harmless, rural pair,
  Void of jealousy or care;
Emblems of the bless'd above,
Sharing pure seraphic love!

By the brook, beneath the shade
Of the lofty poplar laid,
Cheerful strains awake the grove,
Dulcet notes of peace and love.

Say, ye proud, ye rich and great,
Circled round with noise and state,
Real pleasures can ye prove?
No—'tis found in rural love.

Lovely Nymph.

LOVELY nymph now cease to languish,
  Yield not thus thy mind to woe;
Look behind the cloud of anguish,
  Cheering beams of comfort blow,
Cheering beams of comfort blow.

Let enliv'ning hope elate thee,
  Hope that points to fairer skies;
Think the transient ills that wait thee,
  Are but blessings in disguise.
Are but, &c.

Be not by distress dejected:
  Shrink not from affliction's hand;
Falshood is from truth defected,
  By the kind enchantress wand.
By the kind, &c.

Sage instructress, she shall train thee;
  Steady virtue teach thy heart;
Short, but short liv'd pains await thee,
  Endless blessings to impart,
Endless blessings to impart.

A Linnet's Nest.

A LINNET's nest with anxious care,
   Young Strephon one day found me:
When instantly the plunder'd pair,
   With cries came flutt'ring round me;
And is it thus, cries I, unkind,
   You'd raise compassion in me?
Hence, cruel, hence—unless you'd find
   Some better way to win me.

Alas! if to give pain, cry'd he,
   My love for you has wrought me,
I practise but that cruelty,
   You have so often taught me.
If thus the linnet, and his mate,
   Can raise compassion in you;
No more unkindness intimate,
   But let your Strephon join you.

This said, like light'ning, back he flew,
   The mossy nest restoring,
The linnets kept their young in view,
   No more a loss deploring:
Mean while this act, so sweet, so kind,
   Has rais'd affections in me;
And Strephon was well pleas'd to find
   This certain way to win me.

Wisdom's Favorite.

BANISH sorrow grief and folly,
   Thoughts unbend the wrinkling brow;
Hence dull cares and melancholy,
Wine and mirth unite us now.
Bacchus opens all his treasure,
Comus brings us wit and song;
Follow, follow, follow, follow pleasure,
And let's join the jovial song.

Life is short, its but a season;
Time is ever on the wing;
Let's the present moment seize on,
Who knows what the rest may bring?

All my time I now will measure,
All cares I now despise,
Follow, follow, follow, follow pleasure,
To be happy's to be wise.

Wherefore should we thus perplex us,
Why should we not merry be;
Since there's nothing here to vex us;
Drinking sets our hearts all free.
Let's have drinking without measure,
Let's have mirth, what time we have;
Follow, follow, follow, follow pleasure,
There's no drinking in the grave.

The Sailor's Return.

THE busy crew their sails unbending,
  The ship in harbour safe arriv'd,
Jack Oakum (all his perils ending)
  Had made the port where Kitty liv'd.

His rigging—no one dare attack it,
  Tight fore and aft, above, below:
Long-quarter'd shoes, check shirt, blue jacket,
  And trowsers like the driven snow.

His honest heart with pleasure glowing,
  He flew like light'ning to the side;
Scarce had he been a boat's length rowing,
  Before his Kitty he espy'd.

A flowing pennant gaily flutter'd
  From her neat made hat of straw;
Red was her cheek when first she utter'd,
  It was her sailor that she saw.

And now the gazing crew surround her,
  While secure from all alarms,
Swift as a ball from a nine-pounder,
  They dart into each other's arms.

Belinda Blushing.

I SING the beauties that adorn
  Belinda's lovely face,

True at length my vigour's flown,
  I have years to bring decay;
Few the locks that now I own,
  And the few I have are grey;
Yet, old Jerome, thou may'st boast,
  While thy spirits do not tire,
Still beneath thy age's frost
  Glows a spark of youthful fire.
    Oh! the days, &c.

How often must I ask ye?

YOUNG Willy woo'd me long in vain,
  In ev'ry place he met me,
Ah, do you love me, said the swain,
  How often must I ask ye?

I hardly could my love deny,
  For love him I did really;
Why no, you foolish swain, said I,
  How often must I tell ye?

Ah, must I then avoid your view,
  Ah, must I always shun ye!
Then tell me, O my dearest Sue,
  How often must I ask ye?

At length he ask'd my hand, and cried,
  Ah, dearest, do you love me?
Why yes, said I, and often sigh'd,
  How often must I tell ye?

S O N G.

A MASTER I have, and I am his man,
      Galloping dreary dun,
And he'll get a wife as fast as he can,
      With a haily, gaily,
      Gambo raily,
      Giggling,
      Niggling,
Galloping galloway, draggletail dreary dun.

F

I saddled his steed, so fine and so gay,
  Galloping dreary dun:
I mounted my mule, and we rode away,
  With our haily, &c.

We canter'd along until it grew dark,
  Galloping dreary dun;
The nightingale sung instead of the lark,
  With her haily, &c.

We met with a friar, and ask'd him our way,
  Galloping dreary dun;
By the lord, says the friar, you are both astray,
  With your haily, &c.

Our journey, I fear, will do us no good,
  Galloping dreary dun:
We wander alone, like the babes in the wood,
  With our haily, &c.

My master is fighting, and I'll take a peep,
  Galloping dreary dun;
But now I think on it——I'd better go sleep,
  With my haily, &c.

AIR.
Sung in *The Farmer*.

GAD a-mercy! devil's in me,
  All the damsels wish to win me;
Like a maypole round me clutter.
Hanging garlands—fuss and flutter!
Lilting, cap'ring, grinning, smirking;
Pouting, bobbing, winking, jerking;
  Kates and Betties,
  Polls and Letties,
  All were doating, gentle creatures,
  On these features.—
  To their aprons all would pin me,
  Gad-a mercy! devil's in me,
  All the damsels wish to win me.

  Pretty damsels, ugly damsels,
  Black hair'd damsels, red hair'd damsels;
  Six feet damsels, three feet damsels;

Pale fac'd damsels, plump fac'd damsels;
    Small leg'd damsels, thick leg'd damsels;
Pretty, ugly, black hair'd, red hair'd, six feet,
    three feet,
Pale fac'd, plump fac'd, small leg'd, thick leg'd,
    dainty, dowdy;
  All run after me, sir, me;
  For, when pretty fellows we,
  Pretty maids are frank and free.
For their stays taking measure
Of the ladies, oh the pleasure!
Oh, such tempting looks they gi' me;
Wishing of my heart to 'nim me;
Pat and cry, you devil Jemmy!
  Pretty ladies, ugly ladies, &c.

S O N G.

HARK! hark! sweet Lass, the trumpet sounds,
  'Tis honor calls to war;
Now love I leave, perhaps for wounds,
  And beauty for a scar.

But, ah! suppress those rising sighs;
  Ah! check that falling tear:
Lest soft distress, from lovely eyes,
  Create a new born fear.

My life to fame devoted was,
  Before my fair I knew,
And, if I now desert her cause,
  Shall I be worthy you?

It is not fame alone invites;
  Though fame this bosom warms;
My country's violated rights
  Impel my soul to arms.

Oran is no more.
Sung by Mrs. Kemble, in the Benevolent Planter.

IN vain to me the hours of care,
  When ev'ry daily toil is o'er;

In my sad heart no hopes I find,
  For Oran is, alas! no more.
Nor sunny Africa could please,
  Nor friends upon my native shore;
To me the dreary world's a cave,
  For Oran is, alas! no more.

In bow'rs of bliss, beyond the moon,
  The white man says, his sorrow's o'er:
And comforts me with soothing hope,
  Tho' Oran is, alas! no more.

O come then, messenger of death,
  Convey me to the starry shore,
Where I may meet with my true love,
  And never part with Oran more.

SONG.

GO! tuneful bird, that glads the skies,
  To Daphne's window speed thy way,
And there on trembling pinions rise,
And there thy vocal art display:
  And if she deign thy notes to hear,
And if she praise thy matin song,
  Tell her, the sound that sooths her ear,
To Damon's native plains belong.

Tell her in livelier plumes array'd,
The birds from India's groves may shine,
But ask the lovely, partial maid,
What are his notes compar'd with thine?
  Then bid her treat yon witless beau,
And all his flaunting race with scorn,
And lend an ear to Damon's woe,
Who sings her praise, but sings forlorn.

The Barking Barber,
Or, NEW BOW WOW.
A comi-satyri-poetical Lecture on Blockheads.
By Pasq. Shaveblock, Shaver Extraordinary.

YE gents, give ear to me, I pray,
  I am a barking barber,

The best accommodations have,
  Keen razors and hot lather.
Pray walk into my noted shop,
  I shave as clean as any ;
And when Iv'e done it to your mind,
  Will charge you but a penny.
    Bow, wow, wow,
    I am a barking barber.
    Bow, wow, wow,

Ye ragged pates, your hair I'll crop,
  And dress it vastly pretty ;
Or if your blocks are bare, walk in,
  I warrant I can fit ye,
With bag or que, or long pig-tail,
  Or bushy wig, or grizzled,
So well bepowder'd, clean, and white,
  And eke so nicely frizzled.
    Bow, wow, &c.

My shop well furnish'd out with blocks,
  Becomes an exhibition,
Of heads of ev'ry age and kind,
  And every condition :
A lawyer's head without a quirk,
  Without chicane, a proctor's ;
A lady's head without a tongue,
  Without a nostrum doctor's.
    Bow, wow, &c.

A poet's head without a rhyme,
  A wit's too without punning ;
Without a crotchet fidlers head,
  A jockey's without cunning ;
A cuckold's head devoid of horns,
  His wife's without invention ;
A barber's head without his brains,
  And others I could mention.
    Bow, wow, &c.

And let none of the wicked wits
  Despise my occupation,

The greater always shave the less,
　In ev'ry rank and station ;
The rich will ever shave the poor,
　The minister, an't please ye,
Well lathers you with promises,
　Then shaves you mighty easy.
　　Bow, wow, &c.

And shavers clean, I trow there are,
　Of every profession ;
But pardon now, my customers,
　This whimsical digression ;
And walk into my noted shop,
　I shave as clean as any ;
And when I've done it to your mind,
　Will charge you but a penny.
　　Bow, wow, &c.

SONG.

I DREAMT I saw a piteous sight,
　Young Cupid weeping lay,
Until his pretty stars of light,
　Had wept themselves away.

Methought I ask'd him why he wept,
　Mere pity led me on :
He deeply sigh'd and then repli'd,
　Alas ! I am undone.

As I beneath yon myrtle lay,
　Close by Diana's springs,
Amintor stole my bow away,
　And pinion'd both my wings.

Alas ! said I, where's then thy bow,
　Wherewith he wounded me ;
Thou art a god, and such a blow,
　Could come from none but thee.

But if thou wilt revenged be,
　On that ambitious swain,
I'll set thy wings at liberty,
　And thou shalt fly again :
And all the service on my part,
　That I require of thee,

Is that you'd wound Amintor's heart,
  And make him die for me.

The silken fetters I untied,
  And the gay wings display'd,
He mounting, gently fann'd and cry'd,
  Adieu, fond foolish maid!

At that I blush'd and angry grew,
  I should the god believe;
But waking found my dream too true,
  Alas! I was a slave.

The favorite Fishing Duet.

Sung by Mr. Martyr and Mrs. Mountain, in Don Juan.

THUS for men the women fair
  Lay the cunning, cunning snare;
While like fish the men will rove,
And with beauty fall in love.
  What is beauty but a bait,
  Oft' repented when too late.

If too late you seize the prize,
Now display'd before the eyes,
How you'll rue when all is past,
Hymen's hook which holds you fast,
  Ere you marry then beware,
  'Tis a blessing or a snare.

Hopeless Love.

CEASE, tyrant of my flaming bosom, cease,
  Nor force the gentle slumbers from my eyes,
Ah! but again restore my youthful peace,
  And from my breast erase desponding sighs.

May fate relent, nor let me languish here,
  While by her eyes I'm chain'd to gloomy care;
Still for the transient rose I shed a tear,
  And o'er her blushes weep with wild despair.

Impetuous transport pierces while I gaze,
  Corrosive anguish preys upon my mind;
I stand condemn'd to pass unhappy days,
  And leave content and flatt'ring hope behind,

I gr... ...ye in vain,
  Her eyes ... ... ne to my doom ;
Fain would I ... ...ling'ing pain,
  But that will follow ... ...fky tomb.

Fly hope, thou foother, ... wretched breaft,
  Revive no more, nor orin ; t.. gentle aid ;
I mourn, I wander, and I w... nbleft,
  Enflav'd, rejected by a beateuous maid.

The Wandering Sailor.

THE wand'ring failor ploughs the main,
  A competence in life to gain,
Undaunted braves the ftormy feas,
To find, at laft, content and cafe :
In hopes, when toil and danger's o'er,
To anchor on his native fhore.

When winds blow hard, and mountains roll,
And thunders fhake from pole to pole ;
Tho' dreadful waves furrounding foam,
Still flatt'ring fancy wafts him home ;
In hopes, when toil and danger's o'er,
To anchor on his native fhore.

When round the bowl, the jovial crew,
The early fcenes of youth renew ;
Tho' each his fav'rite fair will boaft,
This is the univerfal toaft—
May we, when toil and danger's o'er,
Caft anchor on our native fhore.

S O N G.

BEHOLD on the brow the leaves play in the breeze,
  While cattle calm feed in the vale ;
The church fpires tapering, points thro' the trees,
  As lord of the hill and the dale.

The playful colts fkip after lambs to the brook,
  The brook flow and filent glides :
The furface fo fmooth and fo clear, if you look
  It reflects the gay green on its fides,

By his feather'd feraglio in farm-yard carefs'd,
  The king of the walk dares to crow,
No nabob nor Nimrod enflaving the eaft,
  Such prowefs with beauty can fhew.

Beneath the ftill cow, Nancy preffes the teat,
  Her face like the ruddy fac'd morn :
Loud ftrokes in the barn the ftrong threfhers repeat,
  Or winnow for market the corn.

Induftrious the wives, at the doors of their cots,
  Sit fpinning, drefs'd neatly, tho' coarfe,
To their babes, while unheeding the traveller trots,
  They fhew the fine man and the horfe.

At the heels of the fteed bark the bafe village whelps,
  Each puppy rude echo beftirs ;
But the horfe too high bred, bounds away from their yelps,
  Difregarding the clamour of curs.

Illiberal railers thus envy betray,
  When merit above them they view ;
But genius difdains to turn out of his way,
  Or afford a reply to the crew.

To contempt and difpair fuch infanes we commit ;
  But to generous rivals, a toaft—
May rich men reward honeft fellows of wit—
  Here's a health to thofe dunces hate moft.

The Knights Errant.
Sung by Mr. Edwin, in the Crufade.

Tune—Vicar and Mofes.

KNIGHTS errant of old,
  By their titles we're told,
Thought more of their ftomachs than fame ;
  Each knight from fome treat,
  Some plant or fome meat,
Uncourteoufly borrow'd his name.

SCOTCH——*Tune*—Corn Rigs.

De'il burn you a', quoth St. Andrew,
  Let ither knights gang whistle;
The bonny Scotchman kens his foes,
  And scratches with his thistle.

WELCH——*Tune*—Oh! he de not.

Now, cotsplood, quoth St. David,
        Oh, pless the leek!
Inteed the Welch knight peats the Scot;
        Oh, pless the leek!
Milk, cheese, and curds, and nauny goats,
  With other treats we taffies view,
  And tear and swear, and fight look you,
        Oh, pless the leek!

FRENCH——*Tune*—Young Colin stole my heart.

  St. Dennis di, mes chere amis
  En verite behold a me;
  We French knights dance away, d'ye see,
  And fight for frogs and fricasee.

IRISH——*Tune*—Ally Croaker.

St. Patrick, hot as lightning with whisky and old
    bumbo,
Cry'd out, "Don't bother thus, with noise and hur-
    lo thrumbo;
Here's one with his shilaly will suddenly all beat ye,
Unless your frogs and thistles yield to Pat and his
    potaty.
    Oh, the plump potaty,
    The pretty plump potaty.

ENGLISH——*Tune*—Rule, Britannia.

When errant knights, in proud array,
  Assembled first on Clermont's plain,
This was the burthen of their lay,
  And ev'ry champion join'd the strain:

St. George for ever, for ever live the chief,
St. George, Old England, and roast beef.
  Oh the roast beef of Old England,
  And oh the Old English roast beef!

SONG.

THOU soft flowing Avon! by the silver stream,
  Of subjects immortal thy Shakespeare would
    dream:
The fairies by moonlight dance round his green bed,
For hallow'd the turf is that pillows his head.

Here swains shall be fam'd for their love and their
    truth,
And cheerful old age feel the transports of youth:
For the raptures of fancy here poets shall tread,
For hallow'd the turf is that pillows his head.

The love striken maiden, the sighing young swain,
Here rove without danger and toy without pain:
The sweet bud of beauty no blight shall here dread,
For hollow'd the turf is that pillows his head.

Flow on, silver Avon, in song ever flow,
Be the swans on thy bosom still whiter than snow,
Ever full be thy stream, like his fame may it spred,
And the turf ever hallow'd that pillows his head.

Sterne at the Tomb of Maria.

THE sun shone pale on mountain snow,
  While morn unbarr'd her gate;
Wak'd by his beams, Maria rose,
  To mourn her hapless fate:
In piteous sounds of deepest woe,
  Which echo'd thro' the vale;
Soft as the rising blush of morn,
  Or zephyr's fragrant gale.

All night her shroud before her past,
  The owl cry'd, and raven too;
At eve Maria breath'd her last,
  And prov'd these omens true:

Her spirit's now in heaven repos'd,
  Which here sad vigils kept;
Whose wounds on earth were never clos'd;
  Whose sorrows never slept.

Yet ere I bid my last adieu,
  While in my clay cold bed,
Accept the tear of friendship true,
  Which o'er thy grave I shed;
While life remains, thy hapless love
  In mem'ry e'er shall live;
May'st thou in heav'n those blessings prove,
  Which earth could never give.

SONG.

A FEW years ago, in the days of my Grannum,
  (A worthy good woman as ever broke bread)
What lectures she gave! in the morning began 'em,
  Nor ceas'd till she laid herself down on her bed;
She never declin'd what she once undertook;
    But twisted,
    Persisted,
    Now flatter'd,
    Now spatter'd
And always succeeded, by hook or by crook.

Said she, child, whatever your fate is hereafter,
  If married, if single, if old, or if young,
In madness, in sadness, in tears, or in laughter,
  But follow my maxims you cannot do wrong:
Each passion, each temper, I always could brook;
    When scolded,
    I moulded,
    When heated,
    Retreated,
And manag'd my matters, by hook or by crook.

Ensnar'd by her counsels, I ventur'd to marry,
  And fancy'd a wife, by my grandmother's rules,
Might be taught like a spaniel to fetch and to carry,
  But soon I found out that we both had been fools:

In vain, I show'd madam the wonderful book;
    I coax'd her,
    I box'd her;
    But truly,
    Unruly
Wives cannot be govern'd by hook or by crook.

SONG.

ASPASIA.

By Miss AIKIN.

ASPASIA rolls her sparkling eyes,
    And ev'ry bosom feels her pow'er
The Indians thus view Pœbus rise,
    And gaze in rapture and adore:
Quick to the soul the piercing splendors dart,
Fire ev'ry vein, and melt the coldest heart.

Aspasia speaks—the list'ning croud
    Drink in the sound with greedy ears;
Mute are the giddy and the loud,
    And self-admiring folly hears:
Her wit secures the conquests of her face,
Points ev'ry charm, and heithens ev'ry grace.

Aspasia moves—her well turn'd limbs
    Glide stately with harmonious ease;
Now thro' the mazy dance she swims,
    Like a tall bark o'er summer seas:
'Twas thus Æneas knew the queen of love,
Majestic moving thro' the golden grove.

But ah! how cruel is my lot,
    To doat on one so heav'nly fair!
For, in my humble state forgot,
    Each charm but adds to my despair:
The tuneful swan thus faintly warbling lies,
Looks on his mate, and whilst he sings he dies.

SONG.

COME bustle, bustle, drink about,
  And let us merry be,
Our can is full, we'll pump it out,
  And then all hands to sea.
           And a sailing we will go.

Fine miss at dancing-school is taught
  The minuet to tread;
But we go better when we've brought
  The fore-tack to cat head.

The jockey's call'd to horse, to horse,
  And swiftly rides the race;
But swifter far we shape our course,
  When we are giving chace.

When horns and shouts the forest rend,
  His pack the huntsman cheers;
As loud we hallow when we send,
  A broadside to Monsieurs.

The what's their name, at uproar squall,
  With music fine and soft:
But better sounds our boatswain's call,
  All hands, all hands aloft!

With gold and silver streamers fine
  The ladies rigging shew!
But our ships more grandly shine,
  When prizes home we tow.

What's got at sea we spend on shore,
  With sweethearts, or our wives;
And then, my boys, hoist sail for more!
  Thus pass the sailors lives.
           And a sailing we will go.

What a charming thing's a Battle.

WHAT a charming thing's a battle!
  Trumpets sounding, drums a beating;
Crack, crick, crack, the cannons rattle;
  Ev'ry heart with joy elating;

With what pleasure we are spying,
    From the front, and from the rear,
    Round us in the smoaky air,
Heads and limbs, and bullets flying!
Then the groans of soldiers dying,
    Just like sparrows, as it were,
      At each pop
      Hundreds drop,
While the muskets prittle prattle;
      kill'd and wounded
      Lie confounded;
What a charming thing's a battle!

But the pleasant joke of all,
Is when to close attack we fall,
Like mad bulls each other butting,
Shooting, stabbing, maiming, cutting;
    Horse and foot,
    All go to't;
Kill's the word, both men and cattle;
    Then to plunder;
    Blood and thunder,
What a charming thing's a battle!

Ye Fair possessed.

YE fair possess'd of ev'ry charm,
    To captivate the will,
Whose smiles can rage itself disarm,
    Whose frowns at once can kill:
Say will you deign the verse to hear,
    Where flatt'ry bears no part;
And honest verse, that flows sincere,
    And candid from the heart.

Great is your pow'r; but greater yet,
    Mankind it might engage:
If, as ye all can make a net,
    Ye all could make a cage.
Each nymph a thousand hearts may take;
    For who's to beauty blind?
But to what end a prisoner make,
    Unless you've strength to bind?

Attend the council often told,
  Too often told in vain ;
Learn that best art, the art to hold,
  And lock the lover's chain.
Gamesters to little purpose win,
  Who lose again as fast ;
Tho' beauty may the charm begin,
  'Tis sweetness makes it last.

Ma Chere Amie.

MA Chere Amie, my charming fair,
  Whose smiles can banish ev'ry care ;
In kind compassion smile on me,
Whose only care is love of thee.
               Ma Chere Amie, &c.

Under sweet friendship's sacred name,
My bosom caught the tender flame ;
May friendship in thy bosom be
Converted into love for me.
               Ma Chere Amie, &c.

Together rear'd, together grown,
O let us now unite in one ;
Let pity soften thy decree,
I droop, dear maid, I die for thee.
               Ma Chere Amie, &c.

Mon Cher Ami.

MON Cher Ami, ami tres cher,
  My love shall soothe thy ev'ry care ;
Thou in return shalt smile on me,
Nor ought but love our life shall see.
               Mon Cher Ami, &c.

Under sweet friendship's sacred name,
Thy breast shall still retain the flame,
With which it long has glow'd for me,
Thy constant wedded friend I'll be.
               Mon Cher Ami, &c.

United thus, may ev'ry year,
Thy Lydia grow to thee more dear;
Nor sue for pity more from me,
Nor droop for her who lives for thee.
Mon Cher Ami, &c.

Sandy o'er the Lee.

I WINNA marry one mon but Sandy o'er the lee;
I winna ha the Dominee, for geud he canna be;
But I will ha my Sandy lad, my Sandy o'er the lee.
   For he's aye a kissing, kissing, aye a kissing me.

I will not have the minister, for all his godly looks,
Nor yet will I the lawyer have, for all his wily crooks:
I will not have the plowman lad, nor yet will I the
     miller;
But I will have Sandy lad, without one penny siller.
   For he's aye a kissing, &c.

I will not have the soldier lad, for he gangs to the war;
I will not have the sailor lad, because he smells of tar:
I will not have the lord nor laird, for all their
     mickle gear:
But I will have my Sandy lad, my Sandy o'er the mier.
   For he's aye a kissing, &c.

Virtuous Love.

HOW sweet is love when virtue guides,
   How transient is the mind;
Smooth as the summer's peaceful tides,
   As grateful and as kind.

The morning breaks serenely clear,
   We welcome in the day;
The ev'ning comes without a fear,
   The night our toils repay.

But sad reverse where vice appears,
   With all her scorpion train;
Joyless we pass our prime of years,
   And end a life in pain.

SONG.

Now's the time for mirth and glee,
  Sing, and love, and laugh with me;
Cupid is my theme of story:
'Tis his godship's fame and glory,
  How all yield unto his law!
  Ha! ha! ha! ha! ha! ha! ha!

O'er the grave, and o'er the gay,
Cupid takes his share of pay:
He makes heroes quit their glory;
He's the god most fam'd in story;
  Bending them unto his law!
  Ha! ha! &c.

Sly the urchin deals his darts,
Without pity—piercing hearts:
Cupid triumphs over passions,
Not regarding modes or fashions.
  Firmly fix'd is Cupid's laws!
  Ha! ha! &c.

Some may think these lines not true,
But they're facts—'twixt me and you;
Then, ye maids and men, be wary,
How you meet before you marry:
  Cupid's will is solely law.
  Ha! ha! &c.

The Battle of the Kegs.
By the Honorable F. H. Esquire.
[Tune—Maggy Lawder.]

Gallants attend, and hear a friend,
  Trill forth harmonious ditty:
Strange things I'll tell, which late befel
  In Philadelphia city.

'Twas early day, as poets say,
  Just when the sun was rising;
A soldier stood, on a log of wood,
  And saw a sight surprising.

As in a maze, he stood to gaze,
   The truth can't be denied, sir,
He spy'd a score—of kegs or more,
   Come floating down the tide, sir.

A sailor too, in jerkin blue,
   The strange appearance viewing,
First damn'd his eyes, in great surprise,
   Then said—some mischief's brewing.

These KEGS now hold the rebels bold,
   Pack'd up like pickled herring :
And they're come down t'attack the town,
   In this new way of ferrying.

The soldier flew, the sailor too,
   And scar'd almost to death, sir,
Wore out their shoes, to spread the news,
   And ran till out of breath, sir.

Now up and down, throughout the town,
   Most frantic scenes were acted ;
And some ran here, and some ran there,
   Like men almost distracted.

Some fire cry'd, which some deny'd,
   But said the earth had quaked :
And girls and boys with hideous noise,
   Ran through the town half naked.

* Sir William he, snug as a flea,
   Lay all this time a snoring,
Nor dreamt of harm, as he lay warm,
   In bed with Mrs. L——g.

Now in a fright, he starts upright,
   Awak'd by such a clatter ;
He rubs both eyes, and boldly cries,
   For God's sake what's the matter ?

At his bed-side, he then espy'd
   Sir Erskine† at command sir.
Upon one foot, he had one boot,
   And t'other in his hand, sir.

  * *Sir William Howe.*   † *Sir W. Erskine.*

Arise! arise! Sir Erskine cries:
  The rebels—more's the pity—
Without a boat, are all on float,
  And rang'd before the city.

The motly crew, in vessels new,
  With Satan for their guide, sir,
Pack'd up in bags, or wooden KEGS,
  Come driving down the tide, sir.

Therefore prepare for bloody war;
  These KEGS must all be routed:
Or surely we despis'd shall be;
  And British courage doubted.

The royal band now ready stand,
  All rang'd in dread array, sir,
With stomach stout, to see it out,
  And make a bloody day, sir.

The cannons roar, from shore to shore:
  The small arms make a rattle:
Since wars began, I'm sure no man
  E'er saw so strange a battle.

The rebel* vales, the rebel dales,
  With rebel trees surrounded,
The distant woods, the hills, and floods,
  With rebel echoes sounded.

The fish below, swam to and fro,
  Attack'd from ev'ry quarter:
Why sure, thought they, the devil's to pay
  'Mongst folks above the water.

The KEGS, 'tis said, tho' strongly made,
  Of rebel staves and hoops, sir,
Could not oppose their powerful foes,
  The conqu'ring British troops, sir.

From morn to night these men of might
  Display'd amazing courage;
And when the sun was fairly down,
  Retir'd to sup their porrage.

* *The British officers were so fond of the word rebel, that they often applied it most absurdly.*

An hundred men, with each a pen,
   Or more, upon my word, sir,
It is most true, would be too slow
   Their valour to record, sir.

Such feats did they perform that day
   Upon these wicked KEGS, sir:
That years to come, if they get home,
   They'll make their boast and brags, sir.

SONG.

ONE morning young Roger accosted me thus—
   Come here, pretty maiden, and give me a buss,
Lord! fellow, said I, mind your plough and your cart;
Yes, I thank you for nothing, thank you for nothing, thank you for nothing, with all my heart.

Well, then, to be sure, he grew civil enough,
He gave me a box, with a paper of snuff:
I took it, I own, yet had still so much art,
To cry, thank you for nothing with all my heart.

He said, if so be he might make me his wife—
Good Lord! I was never so dash'd in my life;
Yet could not help laughing to see the fool start,
When I thank'd him for nothing with all my heart.

Soon after, however, he gain'd my consent,
And with him, on Sunday, to chapel I went;
But said, 'twas my goodness more than his desert,
Not to thank him for nothing with all my heart.

The parson cry'd, child, you must after me say,
And then talk'd of honor, and love and *obey*;
But faith, when his reverence came to that part,
There I thank'd him for nothing with all my heart.

At night our brisk neighbours the stocking would throw—
I must not tell tales, but I know what I know;
Young Roger confesses I cur'd all his smart,
And I thank'd him for something with all my heart.

What pleasures can compare, &c.

WHAT pleasures can compare,
 To a sleighing with the fair, [ther?
In the ev'ning, the ev'ning, in cold and frosty wea-
 When rapidly we go,
 As we *gingle* o'er the snow,
And tantarra, huzza! and tantarra, huzza! and
 tantarra sings ev'ry brave fellow.

 When to Kingsbridge we get,
 And the turkey's on the spit, [all sorrow,
And we dance, boys, we dance, boys, and drive away
 'Tis then your milk and tea
 Gives place to " strong sangree,"
And we banish, huzza! and we banish, huzza!
 and we banish the cares of to morrow.

 When the turkey's roasted brown,
 To supper we sit down,
And " keep it up," and " keep it up," sings ev'ry
 jovial fellow,
 With the wine glass in his hand,
 He never makes a stand,
But *guzzles*, huzza! but *guzzles*, huzza! and *guzzles*
 it away until he's mellow.

 Now for York again prepare,
 And the night is cold and clear,
And we're *flowing close*, we're *flowing close*, because
 'tis chilly weather—
 O then what fun we feel,
 When the sleigh it takes a heel.
And we're *huddl'd*, huzza! and we're *huddl'd*, huz-
 za! and we're *huddl'd* brave boys altogether.

 'Tis then the ladies cry,
 O lud!—O dear!—O my!—
And we *scrabble*, boys—we *scrabble* boys, all from
 the snowy weather:
 Then in the sleigh again,
 Do we *scamper* o'er the plain,
And tantarra, huzza! and tantarra, huzza! and
 tantarra sings ev'ry brave fellow.

SONG.

O Sandy, why leav'st thou thy Nelly to mourn?
    Thy presence could ease me,
    When neathing can please me;
Now dowie I sigh on the banks of the burn,
Or thro' the wood, laddie, until thou return.

Tho' woods now are bonny, and mornings are clear,
    While lav'rocks are singing,
    And primroses springing
Yet nane of them pleases mine eye or mine ear,
When thro' the wood, laddie, ye dinna appear.

That I am forsaken, some spare not to tell;
    I am fash'd wi' their scorning,
    Baith ev'ning and morning,
Their jeering gaes aft to my heart wi' a knell.
When thro' the wood, laddie, I wonder mysell.

Then stay, my dear Sandy, nae longer away;
    But quick as an arrow,
    Haste here to thy marrow,
Wha's living in languor till that happy day,
When thro' the wood, laddie, we'll dance, sing, and play.

A Hunting Song.

HARK! forward, away, my brave boys to the chace,
    To the joys that sweet exercise yield;
The bright ruddy morning breaks on us apace,
    And invites to the sports of the field.
Hark! forward's the cry, and cheerful the morn,
Then follow the hounds and the merry ton'd horn.

No music can equal the hounds in full cry;
    Hark! they open, then hasten away;
O'er hill, dale and valley, with vigour we fly,
    While pursuing the sports of the day.
      Hark! forward's the cry, &c.

With the sports of the field, no joys can compare,
    To pleasure's light footsteps we trace;

We run down dull sloth, and we distance old care,
'Rosy health we o'ertake in the chace.
Hark! forward's the cry, &c.

SONG.

THAT I might not be plagu'd with the nonsense of men,
I promis'd my mother, again and again,
To say as she bids me wherever I go,
And to all that they ask, or would have, tell 'em no.

I really believe I have frighten'd a score;
They'll want to be with me, I warrant, no more;
And I own I'm not sorry for serving them so;
Were the same thing to do, I again should say no.

For a shepherd I like with more courage and art,
Who won't let me alone, though I bid him depart;
Such questions he puts, since I answer him so,
That he makes me mean yes, thro' words are still no.

He ask'd, did I hate him, or think him too plain?
(Let me die if he is not a clever young swain.)
If he ventur'd a kiss, if I from him would go,
Then he press'd my young lips, while I blush'd, and said no.

He ask'd if my heart to another was gone?
If I'd have him to leave me, or cease to love on?
If I meant my life long to answer him so?
I faulter'd, and sigh'd, and reply'd to him, no.

This morning an end to his courtship he made;
Will Phillis live longer a virgin? he said;
If I press you to church, will you scruple to go?
In a hearty good humour I answer'd, no, no.

SONG.

Tune—Top-sails shivers in the wind.

'TWAS at the break of day we spy'd
    The signal to unmoor,
Which sleepless Caroline descry'd,
    Sweet maid! from New-York shore;
The fresh'ning gale at length arose,
    Her heart began to swell,
Nor could cold fear the thought oppose,
    Of bidding me farewell!

In open boat the maid of worth,
    Soon reach'd our vessel's side:
Soon too she found her William's birth,
    But sought me not to chide:
' Go,' she exclaim'd, ' for fame's a cause
    A female should approve,
' For who that's true to honor's laws
    ' Is ever false to love!

' My heart is loyal, scorns to fear,
    ' Nor will it even fail.
' Tho' war's unequal wild career,
    ' Should William's life assail;
' Tho' death 'gainst thee exert his sway.
    ' Oh, trust me, but the dart
' That woundeth thee, will find its way
    ' To Caroline's true heart.

' Should conquest in fair form array'd,
    ' Thy loyal efforts crown,
' In New-York will be found a maid,
    ' That lives for thee alone.'
May girls with hearts so firm and true,
    To love and glory's cause,
Meet the reward they have in view,
    The meed of free applause.

When Orpheus went down, &c.

WHEN Orpheus went down to the regions below,
  Which men are forbidden to see;
He tun'd up his lyre, as old histories show,
  To let his Eurydice free.

All hell was astonish'd, a person so wise
  Should rashly endanger his life,
And venture so far; but how vast their surprise,
  When they heard that he came for his wife!

To find out a punishment due for his fault
  Old Pluto long puzzled his brain,
But hell had not torments sufficient he thought,
  So he gave him his wife back again.

But pity succeeding soon vanquish'd his heart,
  And pleas'd with his playing so well,
He took her again in reward of his art,
  Such merit had music in hell.

The Crying and Laughing Song.

WHEN I wake with painful brow,
  Ere the cock begins to crow,
Tossing, tumbling in my bed,
Aching heart, and aching head,
Pond'ring over human ills,
Cruel bailiffs, taylors bills,
Flush and pam thrown up at loo,
When those sorrows strike my view,
    I cry, - - - -
And to stop the gushing tear,
Wipe it with the pillow bear.

But when sportive evening comes,
Routs, ridottos, balls, and drums,
Casinos here, festinos there,
Mirth and pastime ev'ry where.

Seated by a sprightly lass,
Smiling with a smiling glass;

When these pleasures are my lot,
Taylors, bailiffs, all forgot,
    I laugh, - - - -
Careless what may then befall,
Thus I shake my sides at all.

Then again when I peruse,
O'er my tea the morning news,
Dismal tales of plunder'd houses,
Wanton wives and cuckold spouses;
When I read of money lent,
At sixteen and half per cent.
    I cry, - - - -

But if e'er the muffin's gone,
Simp'ring enter honest John,
' Sir, Miss Lucy's at the door,
' Waiting in a chaise and four,'
Instant vanish all my cares,
Swift I scamper down the stairs,
    And laugh, - - - -

So may this indulgent throng,
Who now smiling grace my song,
Never more cry oh! oh! la!
But join with me in ha! ha! ha!

Let the Toast pass.

HERE's to the maid of bashful fifteen,
 Likewise to the widow of fifty;
Here's to the bold and extravagant queen,
 And here's to the house wife that's thrifty.
  Let the toast pass,
  Drink to the lass,
I warrant she'll prove an excuse for the glass.

Here's to the maiden whose dimples we prize,
 And likewise to her that has none, sir:
Here's to the maid with a pair of blue eyes,
 And here's to her that's but one, sir.
  Let the toast pass, &c.

Here's to the maid with a bosom of snow,
 And to her that's as brown as a berry;
And here's to the wife with a face full of woe,
 And here's to the girl that is merry.
  Let the toast pass, &c.

Let her be clumsy, or let her be slim,
 Young or ancient I care not a feather;
So fill the pint bumper quite up to the brim,
 And e'en let us toast them together.
  Let the toast pass, &c.

A Toast.

Tune—*Ye Lads who approve.*

WHEN running life's race,
 We gallop apace,
Each strive to be first at the post;
 Mount hope with catch-weights,
 For fame's give-and-take plates,
And pray what is fame but a toast?

 The taste of our days
 Is poaching for praise,
All men of their services boast;
 The ladies by dress,
 The same ardour express,
Each wou'd if she cou'd be a toast.

 Both sexes agree,
 Over wine to be free,
For freedom's an American's boast;
 As freely we think,
 So as freely we drink,
And a sentiment give for a toast.

 What is life? prithee say,
 But a glass and away,
While health is our ruddy fac'd host;
 But when we abuse him,
 We're certain to lose him,
By taking too much of a toast.

These common-place rhimes
Suit common-place times.
Who now can of genius boaſt ?
Why, really, I think
'Tis a ſcience to drink,
And there's genius in giving a toaſt.

Even politics fail,
Altercation grows ſtale,
Of what now can either ſide boaſt ?
No matter to us,
All their farce and their fuſs,
Deſerves not the name of a toaſt.

The riots and routs
Of the ins and the outs,
Is only a news-paper roaſt;
Of criket I ſing,
In and out there's the thing,
And there I'll attempt a new toaſt.

May our innings be long,
May our howling be ſtrong,
Middle-wicket I chuſe for my poſt;
Come, bumper away,
'Twixt the ſtumps your balls play,
And win the game love—that's the toaſt.

The Jolly Miller.

THERE was a jolly miller once liv'd on the river Dee;
He danc'd and ſung from morn 'till night, no lark ſo blithe as he.
And this the burthen of his ſong for ever us'd to be,
I care for no body, no, not I, if no body cares for me.

I live by my mill, God bleſs her! ſhe's kindred, child, and wife;
I would not change my ſtation for any other in life.
No lawyer, ſurgeon, or doctor, e'er had a groat from me. [me.
I care for no body, no, not I, if no body cares for

When spring begins its merry career, oh! how his
   heart grows gay!   [sad decay,
No summer's drouth alarms his fears, no winters
No foresight marrs the miller's joy, who's wont to
   sing and say,   [to day.
Let others toil from year to year, I live from day

Thus, like the miller bold and free, let us rejoice
   and sing;   [on the wing.
The days of youth are made for glee, and time is
This song shall pass from me to thee, along this jo-
   vial ring: [we sing.
Let heart and voice and all agree to say long may

Blow high, blow low.

BLOW high, blow low, let tempests tear
 The mainmast by the board,
My heart with thoughts of thee my dear,
 And love well stor'd,
Shall brave all danger, scorn all fear,
The roaring winds, the raging seas
 In hopes on shore,
 To be once more
Safe moor'd with thee.

Aloft, while mountains high we go,
 The whistling winds that scud along,
And the surge roaring from below,
 Shall my signal be to think on thee,
 Shall my signal be
 To think on thee.
And this shall be my song,
 Blow high, &c.

And on that night when all the crew
 The mem'ry of their former lives
O'er flowing cans of flip renew,
 And drink their sweethearts and their wives,
I'll heave a sigh, I'll heave a sigh
 And think on thee;
 And as the ship rolls thro' the sea,
The burden of my song shall be.
 Blow high, &c.

As on a Summer's Day.

AS on a summer's day,
In the greenwood shade I lay,
  The maid that I lov'd,
  As her fancy mov'd,
Came walking forth that way.

And as she passed by,
With a scornful glance of her eye,
  What a shame, quoth she,
  For a swain must it be,
Like a lazy loon for to lie?

And dost thou nothing heed
What pan our God has decreed
  What a prize to day
  Shall be given away,
To the sweetest shepherd's reed.

There's not a single swain,
Of all this fruitful plain,
  But with hopes and fears,
  Now busily prepares
The bonny boon to gain.

Shall another maiden shine
In brighter array than thine
  Up, up, dull swain,
  Tune thy pipe once again
And make the garland mine.

Alas! my love, I cry'd,
What avails this courtly pride?
  Since thy dear desert
  Is written in my heart,
What is all the world beside?

To me thou art more gay
In this homely russet gray,
  Than the nymphs of our green,
  So trim and so sheen,
Or the brightest queen of May.

What tho' my fortune frown,
And deny thee a silkin gown ;
   My own dear maid,
     Be content with this shade
And a shepherd all thy own.

Jolly Mortals.

JOLLY mortals fill your glasses,
  Noble deeds are done by wine ;
Scorn the nymph and all her graces,
  Who'd for love or beauty pine ?

Look within the bowl that's flowing,
  And a thousand charms you'll find,
More than Phillis has, tho' going
  In the moment to be kind.

Alexander hated thinking,
  Drank about at council board :
He subdu'd the world by drinking
  More than by his conqu'ring sword.

The Joys of Sleighing.

OF all the fine things that the gay celebrate,
  And the many odd fancies that come from
    each pate,
Sure its matter of wonder that none ere refound
The circle of joys that in sleighing abound.

There are some who in phaeton glory to roll,
Whilst others in chariots expand the whole soul,
To bestride prancing horses full many may please ;
But the pleasures of sleighing are greater than these.

Musidora, miss Mira, and all the gay throng,
In exchange for a sleighing will give you a song ;
They will leave a dear ball, concerto or play,
And vow that no music's as sweet as a sleigh.

Then strike a bold stroke, gain their hearts while
    you can,
The greater gallant, the more favorite man.
'Tis not whining nor pining that carries the day :
So away with such nonsense, and out with the sleigh!

A Bacchanalian Silk.

DEAR Tom, this brown jug, that now foams
    with mild ale,
(In which I will drink to sweet Nan of the Vale)
Was once Toby Philpot, a thirsty old soul,
As e'er drank a bottle, or fathom'd a bowl;
In boozing about 'twas his praise to excel,
And among jolly topers he bore off the bell.

It chanc'd, as in dog-days he sat at his ease,
In his flow'r-woven arbour, as gay as you please,
With a friend and a pipe, puffing sorrow away,
And with honest old stingo was soaking his clay;
His breath-doors of life on a sudden was shut,
And he died, full as big as a Dorcester butt.

His body when long in the ground it had lain,
And time into clay had desolv'd it again,
A potter found out, in its cover so snug,
And with part of fat Toby I form'd this brown jug:
Now sacred to friendship, to mirth and mild ale;
So here's to my lovely sweet Nan of the Vale.

SAY, PHŒBE, WHY, &c.

Written by *Mr. Pope*, but not published in his works.

SAY Phœbe why is gentle love
    A stranger to to that mind,
Which pity and esteem can move,
    Which can be just and kind?

Is it because you fear to prove
    The ills that love molest,
The ... cares, the sighs that move
    The captivated breast?

Alas! by some degrees of woe
    We ev'ry bliss obtain;
That heart can ne'er a transport know,
    That never felt a pain.

Dusky Night.

THE dusky night rides down the sky,
 And ushers in the morn ;
The hounds all join in jovial cry,
 The huntsman winds his horn.
    And a hunting we will go, &c.

The wife around her husband throws
 Her arms to make him stay ;
My dear, it rains, it hails, it snows!
 You cannot hunt to-day.
    Yet a hunting, &c.

Away they fly to 'scape the rout,
 Their steeds they soundly switch ;
Some are thrown in, some are thrown out,
 And some thrown in the ditch.
    Yet a hunting, &c.

At last from strength to faintness worn,
 Poor reynard ceases flight ;
Then weary homeward we return,
 And drink away the night.
    And a drinking, &c.

Go Plaintive Sounds.

GO plaintive sounds! and to the fair
 My secret wounds impart;
Tell all I hope, tell all I fear,
 Each motion in my heart.

But she, methinks, is list'ning now
 To some enchanting strain ;
The smile that triumphs o'er his brow
 Seems not to heed my pain.

Yes, plaintive sounds ! yet, yet delay,
 Howe'er my love repine ;
Let that gay minute pass away,
 The next perhaps is thine.

Yes, plaintive sounds ! no longer cross;
 Your grief shall soon be o'er ;

Her cheek, undimpled now, has loſt
  The ſmile it lately wore.

Yes, plaintive ſounds! ſhe now is yours,
  'Tis now your time to move;
Eſſay to ſoften all her powers,
  And be that ſoftneſs, love.

Ceaſe, plaintive ſounds! your taſk is done;
  That anxious tender air
Proves o'er her heart the conqueſt won;
  I ſee you melting there.

Return, ye ſmiles, return again,
  Return each ſprightly grace;
I yield up to your charming reign
  All that enchanting face.

I take no outward ſhew amiſs.
  Rove where you will, her eyes;
Still let her ſmiles each ſhepherd bleſs,
  So ſhe but hear my ſighs.

A Courting I went to my Love.

A Courting I went to my love,
  Who is ſweeter than roſes in May:
And when I came to her by Jove,
  The devil a word could I ſay.

I walk'd with her into the garden,
  There fully intending to woo her!
But may I ne'er be worth a farthing,
  If of love I ſaid any thing to her.

I claſp'd her hand cloſe to my breaſt,
  While my heart was as light as a feather
Yet nothing I ſaid, I proteſt,
  But—madam, 'tis very fine weather.

To an arbor I did her attend,
  She aſk'd me to come and ſit by her:
I crept to the furthermoſt end,
  For I was afraid to come nigh her.

I aſk'd her which way was the wind,
  For I thought in ſome talk we muſt enter;

Why, sir (she answer'd, and grinn'd)
  Have you just sent your wits for a venture?
Then I follow'd her into the house,
  There I vow'd I my passion would try;
But there I was as still as a mouse:
  Oh! what a dull booby was I!

ANNA'S URN.—Sung in—*The Lord of the Manor.*

ENCOMPASS'D in an angel's frame,
  An angel's virtues lay;
Too soon did heav'n assert its claim,
  And call'd its own away.
My Anna's worth, my Anna's charms,
  Can never more return:
What then shall fill these widow'd arms,
  Ah me! my Anna's urn.
Can I forget that bliss refin'd,
  Which, blest with her, I knew?
Our hearts, in sacred bonds entwin'd,
  Were bound by love too true.
That rural train which once were us'd
  In festive dance to turn,
So pleas'd, when Anna they amus'd,
  Now weeping deck her urn.
The soul escaping from its chain,
  She clasp'd me to her breast,
To part with thee is all my pain,
  She cry'd, then sunk to rest.
While mem'ry shall her feat retain,
  From beauteous Anna torn,
My heart shall breathe in ceaseless strain,
  Of sorrow o'er her urn.
There, with the earliest dawn, a dove
  Laments her murder'd mate;
There Philomela, lost to love,
  Tells the pale moon her fate.
With yew and ivy round me spread,
  My Anna there I'll mourn;
For all my soul, now she is dead,
  Concenters in her urn.

SONG.

Sung at the celebration of the Fourth of July, 1793, in Paſſyunk Townſhip, by a Select Company.

Tune—Jeho Doboin.

WEST of th' old Atlantic, firm Liberty ſtands!
    Hov'ring Fame juſt alighted, ſupported by bands
Of native free born, who ſtill loudly ſing,
" We'll defend our juſt rights againſt tyrant and king."   *Chorus, Taral Laddey, &c.*

George the Third ſhe diſowns, and his proud lordly cheats,
His murdering legions and half famiſh'd fleets,
Who flew thro' the Jerſies, with fear quite diſmay'd,
Altho' they much boaſted that " fighting's their trade."   *Chorus.*

Our juſt rights to aſſert hath the Congreſs oft tried,
Whoſe wiſdom and ſtrength our opponents deride;
And ſtill, madly, in rage, their weak thunders are hurl'd,
To bring us on our knees, and to bully the world.   *Chorus.*

Too haughty to quit, yet too weak to withſtand,
They ſkulk to their ſhips and leave us the firm land,
In dread leſt they ſhare, what Jack Burgoyne did feel,
And the game be quite loſt, as poor Jack loſt his deal.   *Chorus.*

Jack, thinking of Cribbage, All Fours, or of Putt,
With a dexterous hand he did ſhuffle and cut;
And when likely to loſe (like a ſharper they ſay)
Did attempt to reneague—I mean run-away.   *Chorus.*

I

But watched so closely, he could not play booty,
Yet, to cheat he fain would (for George 'twas his duty)
A great bet depending on that single game,
Dominion and honor, destruction and shame.
          Chorus.

He examin'd with care his most critical hand,
At a loss (if 't were better) to beg or to stand;
His tricks reckoned up, for all sharpers can jangle,
Then kick'd up a dust for his favourite wrangle.
          Chorus.

'Twas diamond cut diamond, spades were of no use,
But to dig up the way to surrender or truce,
For he dreaded the hand that dealt out such thumps,
As the hearts were run out, and clubs were then trumps.   Chorus.

Thus he met with the rubbers, as the game it turn'd out,
Poor Jack, altho' beat, made a terrible rout;
Complain'd he was cheated, yet, pompously talks,
Quit the game with a curse, while he rubb'd out the chalks.   Chorus.

But see a cloud burst, and four Cherubs appear!
Loud trumpeting peace, while in blood to their ears,
With Bulls and with pardons, for us on submission,
To lull us and gull us, by their *sham commission*.
          Chorus.

The haughty great George, then to peace is now prone,
A bully, when match'd, soon can alter his tone;
'Tis the act of a Briton to bluster and threaten,
Hang his tail like a puppy, when handsomely beaten.   Chorus.

Charge your glasses lip high, to brave WASHING-
  TON sing,
To the Union so glorious, United States ring;
May their counsels in wisdom and valour unite,
And the men ne'er be wrong, who, yet so far are
  right.   Chorus.

The great Doctor FRANKLIN the next glass must
  claim,
Whose electrical rod struck terror and shame;
Like Moses who caus'd Pharaoh's heart strings to
  grumble,
Shock'd George and his throne, his magicians made
  humble.   Chorus.

To Gates and to Lincoln, in bumpers we'll join,
And to all our brave troops who took gambl'ing
  Burgoyne;
May their luck still increase, as they've turn'd up
  one Jack,
To cut and turn up all the *Knaves in the Pack*.
                                         Chorus.

SONG.—*July* 4.
Tune—*Rule Britannia, &c.*

WHEN America first, at Heaven's command,
  Arose to curb old Britain's pride,
Drive Tyranny from out the land,
Fair Freedom echo'd far and wide.
  " Rouse America, rouse, be free,
  For Nature's God gave Liberty."

To thee belongs the peaceful reign;
Thy cities shall with commerce flow;
 Thy ships explore the boundless main,
And plenty laugh at every foe,
    Hail America! thou art free.
    The universe shall trade with thee.

The nations not so blest as we,
Shall in their turns to tyrants fall,
  Whilst thou shalt rise triumphantly,
The glory and the joy of all.
    Hail America! thou art free,
    The slavish Britons envy thee.

Still more majestic shalt thou rise,
Upheld by France's friendly wing,
  And view thy commerce—swift it flies,
As Neptune's car—old ocean's king.
    Hail America! thou art free,
    The sea-gods! all, are friends to thee.

Each haughty tyrant's sordid yoke,
Their vain attempts to bend thee down,
  Shall fall beneath thy manly stroke,
With broken sceptre and lost crown!
    Hail America! thou art free,
    Thou'st fought and bled for liberty.

The Muses on seraphic wing,
Shall to thy happy coasts repair,
  With laurel crown'd, and chant and sing,
To manly hearts, who guard the free.
    Smile America! thou art Fair,
    The Muses all are friends to thee.

Congratulating bowls go round,
To WASHINGTON, and never cease;
  In shouts triumph, with music crown'd,
To Safety, Liberty, and Peace.
    Smile America! thou art free,
    In spite of George and tyranny.

For Freedom! hearts and hands we'll join,
Blest Independence, hope and joy!
  The theme, how noble, how divine!
Join, join the annual feu-de-joye.
    Smile America! thou art free,
    A race of Heroes springs from thee,

SONG.

Tune—God Save Great George, &c.

FAME, let thy trumpet found,
  Tell all the world around,
          Columbia's free!
Tell Germaine, North and Bute,
And every other brute,
  Tyrannic George won't suit
          Her liberty.

Up forth in joyful found,
From camp to camp refound,
          Washington's fame.
His feats spread far and near,
That friends and foes may hear,
And Britain's island fear
          Washington's name.

A glorious race he's run,
The immortal Washington,
          To make us free.
He vanquish'd all our foes,
The clumsy Hessian knows,
And all who dar'd t' oppose,
          Our liberty.

The fifteen linked chain,
In union we'll maintain,
          'Till time's no more.
Hark! how the valleys ring,
" Slav'ry! detested thing,
To hell with rapid wing,
          Quit, quit our shore."

God grant since Washington,
Our liberty has won,
          Sent from above,

Still may his gallant arm,
Secure us from all harm,
Our grateful bosoms warm,
    With joy and love.

The bloody George in vain
May forge a stronger chain,
    The deed is done!
A greater George than he,
Hath set Columbia free;
Immortaliz'd shall be,
    George WASHINGTON.

S O N G.—*July 4.*
Tune—Rule Britannia, &c.

WHEN exil'd *Freedom*, forc'd to roam,
 Sought refuge on *Columbia*'s shores,
The lovely wand'rer found a home,
And this the *Day* that made *Her* ours.
 Hail Columbia! Columbia hail! to THEE
 The praise is due, that MAN IS FREE.

In her defence, the patriot crowd,
Rush'd to the field, and frown'd on Death;
They seal'd her triumphs with their blood,
And hail'd her with their dying breath.
 Hail Columbia, &c.

'Twas not Columbia's cause alone;
At stake, the Rights of Mankind lay:
That cause, shall distant nations own,
And hail, with joy, this festive day.
 Hail Columbia, &c.

'Tis the World's Day-Star, and shall last
Till Slav'ry's shadows be withdrawn:
And lo! that night is almost past,
And *Europe's* day begins to dawn.
 Hail Columbia, &c.

"Hail then the glorious day,
"Which rous'd the slumb'ring world!"
Henceforth, &c.

Difdaining tyrant frowns,
  Fair freedom fled her home,
Forfook European crowns,
  Through weftern wilds to roam;
Then firft Columbia's virgin breaft
  Inhal'd the facred fire,
Which flafh'd, though long fuppreft,
  And bade the world admire.

Sweet mountain nymph, by thee,
  In arts of peace we fhone,
O'erfhadow'd by the tree,
  The fruits were all our own:
But when ambition frown'd in arms,
  To chain Columbia's fwains,
To war thy voice gave charms,
  And fill'd embattled plains.

Rous'd by thy gen'rous fire,
  Columbia's untaught fons
Made e'en the brave retire
  —So fatal were their guns:
But when confed'rate Gallia join'd
  Her war-worn heroes too,
The Lion ftrong declin'd
  The combat, and withdrew.

Since peace with plenty reigns,
  Let Freedom's fons rejoice!
For now fhe makes thefe plains
  Her refidence of choice—
In fair Columbia's bofom rears
  Her high and awful throne,
From thence her will declares,
  And makes mankind her own.

See ally'd Gallia burns
  To be acknowledg'd thine,

And luckless Belgia mourns
  Before thy sacred shrine—
Oh, hear indulgent nymph, yet hear
  Thy suppliant son's request!
O'er both thy banner rear,
  And smile their fears to rest!

Yet one request remains,
  The dearest thou canst give,
Let him who still sustains
  Our new-born empire, live.
Still bless, heav'n-born, his latest hour!
  Oh! guard thy darling son!
Protected by thy pow'r,
  Long live great WASHINGTON!

Still may the circling glass,
  Whilst time pursues his round,
Whene'er this day shall pass,
  With Washington be crown'd:
" By him Oppression lost her sway,
  " From Pride's high summit hurl'd,
" Hail him, and hail the day
  " Which rous'd the slumb'ring world!"

SONG.—*From the French.*
Tune—Marseilles March.

YE sons of France, away to glory,
  Hark, hark, what myriads bid you rise,
Your children, wives and grandsires hoary;
  Behold their tears, and hear their cries.
Shall hateful tyrants mischief breeding,
  With hireling hosts, a ruffian band,
  Affright and desolate the land.
While peace and liberty lie bleeding;
  To arms, to arms, ye brave,
    The avenging sword unsheath.
  March on, march on, all hearts resolv'd
    On victory or death.

Now, now the dangerous storm is rolling,
  Which treach'rous kings, confederates, rise,
The dogs of war, let loose, are howling,
  And lo! our fields and cities blaze;
And shall we basely view the ruin,
  While lawless foes with guilty pride,
  Spread desolation far and wide,
With crimes and blood their hands imbruing.
    To arms, ye brave, &c.

With luxury and pride surrounded,
  The vile insatiate despots dare,
From thirst of power and gold unbounded,
  To meet and vend the light and air;
Like beasts of burden would they load us,
  Like Gods, would bid their slaves adore;
  But man is man, and who is more?
Then, shall they longer lash and goad us?
    To arms, ye brave, &c.

O liberty! can man resign thee,
  Once having felt thy gen'rous flame?
Can dungeons, bolts, and bars confine thee
  Or whips thy noble spirit tame?
Too long the world has wept, bewailing
  That falsehood's dagger, tyrants wield;
  But freedom is our word and shield,
And all their arts are unavailing.
    To arms, ye brave, &c.

―――

LIBERTY TREE.

IN a chariot of light from the regions of day,
  The Goddess of Liberty came,
Ten thousand celestials illumined her way,
  And Order conducted the dame.

K

A fair buding branch from the gardens above,
  Where millions with millions agree,
She brought in her hand as a pledge of her love,
  And the plant she call'd *Liberty Tree.*

The celestial exotic stuck deep in the ground,
  Like a native it flourish'd and bore,
The fame of its fruit drew the nations around,
  For to search out its peaceable shore;
Unmindful of names and distinctions they came,
  For freemen like brothers agree,
With one spirit endued, they all friendship pursued,
  And their temple was Liberty Tree.

Beneath its fair branches the patriarchs of old,
  Their bread with contentment did eat,
Unvext with the troubles of silver and gold,
  Or the cares of the grand and the great;
With timber and tar they old England supply'd,
  And supported her power on sea;
Her battles they fought without getting a groat,
  For the honor of Liberty Tree.

But give ear, O ye swains, to a tale most profane,
  How all these tyrannical powers,
King, Commons and Lords, did together combine,
  To destroy this fine garden of flowers:
From the east to the west blow the trumpet to arms,
  Thro' the land let the sound of it flee,
That the brave may all hear and unite with a cheer
  In defence of their Liberty Tree.

ODE TO LIBERTY.
Tune—Liberty Tree.

O'ER the vine-cover'd hills and gay regions of France,
  See the day-star of Liberty rise;

Through the clouds of detraction, unwearied advance,
    And hold a new course through the skies.
An effulgence so mild, with a lustre so bright,
    All Europe with wonder surveys;
And from desarts of darkness, and dungeons of night,
    Contends for a share of the blaze.

Let Burke, like a bat, from its splendor retire,
    A splendor—too strong for his eyes;
Let pedants and fools his effusions admire,
    Entrapt in his cobwebs like flies:
Shall phrenzy and sophistry hope to prevail
    Where reason opposes her weight?
When the welfare of millions is hung in the scale,
    And the balance yet trembles with fate?

Ah! who midst the horrors of night would abide,
    That can taste the pure breezes of morn;
Or who, that has drank of the chrystaline tide,
    To the feculent flood would return?
When the bosom of beauty the throbbing heart meets,
    Ah! who can the transport decline!
Or who that has tasted of liberty's sweets,
    The prize, but with life would resign?

[The despots combin'd shall destruction inhale,
    From the air in each pelucid stream,
While Fame from her trump shall infuse in the gale,
    " Their attempt shall depart like a dream:
" Emanations celestial, descend on the world,
    " And thro' France give th' electrical shock;
" While slavery and chains to destruction are hurl'd,
    " Freedom's temple stands firm on the rock."]

But 'tis over—high heaven the decision approves—
    Oppression has struggled in vain;
To the hell she has form'd superstition removes,
    And tyranny bites its own chain.
In the records of time a new æra unfolds,
    All nature exults in its birth—
His creation, benign, the Creator beholds,
    And gives a new charter to earth.

O catch its high import, ye winds as ye blow!
    O bear it, ye waves, as ye roll!
From the regions that feel the sun's vertical glow,
    To the farthest extremes of the pole!
Equal rights, equal laws to the nations around,
    Peace and *Friendship* its precepts impart,
And wherever the footsteps of *Man* shall be found,
    May he bind the decree on his heart.

FRANCE and FREEDOM.
An ODE.
Tune—Handell's Clarinet.

LIFT aloft the trumpet,
    Oh sound, sound Fame,
The heavenly decree,
    That the world shall be free,
While sweet Liberty,
    And Equality,
Consume tyranny, with freedom's awful sacred flame.
    From the west to the east let the tidings roll,
To charm each free-born soul:
Shout, shout for *France*—the cap display,
Fair Freedom greets her natal day;
Mankind, shall loathe the tyrant's hateful baneful
    name.

Raise the joyful chorus,
        High prize the glass;
'Tis a boon from on high,
To our noble ally;
'Tis a gracious beheft,
On its tour from the west,
To kill slavery, while despots to oblivion pass.
  Good will from heaven to man descends;
  The enfranchis'd world are friends;
  Shout, shout, and make a joyful noise,
  'Tis *France* and *Freedom* crowns our joys:
He who denies the toast we'll banish from our class.

On SOCIETY.

Tune—Bunker's Hill.

HAIL, social converse! source of purest plea-
    sure,
Sweet and reviving as the rosy morning,
When first the day-star gilds the face of nature
              With his blest radience.

Hail sacred friendship! fraught with choicest bless-
    ings,
Where souls congenial taste thy sacred union,
Bound by the cement of refin'd affection,
            Founded on virtue.

Truth, heavenly goddess, baffles our researches,
While painful languor springs from ceaseless study,
Welcome sweet converse, kind refreshing cordial,
            Ever delightful.

Thy cheering influence soothes the ruffled passion,
While pale misfortune sinks the weary spirits,
So the clouds vanish, where the radient sun-beams
           Shine in full splendour.

If thus exalted thy enliv'ning pleasure,
In these dull regions, how sublimely glorious,
Mid the bright mansions, where immortal friendship
                Blooms in perfection.

ENGLISH CA IRA.

Tune—Ballinamona, Oro.

WHY give to your tyrants the laurel of fame?
    For honest *Wat Tyler* more glory can claim;
When ruffians presum'd honest maidens to vex,
Wat felt like a man, and defended the sex.
        Sing Ca Ira, Ca Ira, ah! ah!
          Ca Ira, Ca Ira, ah! ah!
          Ca Ira, Ca Ira, ah! ah!
    Defenders of women for me!

Let the sons of oppression eternally sing
The praise of nobility, prelates, and king,
We scorn the distinction that despots create,
But respect worthy fellows whatever their state.
        Sing Ca Ira, Ca Ira, ah! ah!
          Ca Ira, Ca Ira, ah! ah!
    All worthy good fellows for me!

Tom Paine, a true Englishman high in renown,
Shews that plunder's the system of minister and
    crown,
They thrive by degrading the people's degree—
But we know that mankind has a right to be free.
        Sing Ca Ira, Ca Ira, ah! ah!
          Ca Ira, Ca Ira, ah! ah!
    The rights of the people for me!

The peer and the pedlar but differ in name,
If their virtues are equal—their nature's the same;

Then of *titles*, and orders, we've sure had enough;
They're the gewgaws of folly, contemptible stuff.
    Sing Ca Ira, Ca Ira, ah! ah!
      Ca Ira, Ca Ira, ah! ah!
    No gewgaws of folly for me!

True light pholosophic their emptiness shews,
As vacant as bubbles that infancy blows;
On blockheads and villains they frequently fall,
But the title of *Man* is the best after all.
    Sing Ca Ira, Ca Ira, ah! ah!
      Ca Ira, Ca Ira, ah! ah!
    No third oppressors for me!

The world has too long been deceiv'd by the *few*,
Who have dar'd with derision the *many* to view,
And cruelly mocking pale poverty's tear,
Have torn from the helpless e'en millions a year.
    Sing Ca Ira, Ca Ira, ah! ah!
      Ca Ira, Ca Ira, ah! ah!
    No robbing the helpless for me!

Yet, in Britain, each year, many millions are paid,
By those who subsist by the plough and the spade;
For the peasants are stripp'd of their daily support,
To extend the corruption and pride of a court.
    Sing Ca Ira, Ca Ira, ah! ah!
      Ca Ira, Ca Ira, ah! ah!
    No pride and corruption for me!

And when they in abject condition are left,
Of their earnings, of justice, of comfort bereft,
Curs'd tyrants their *low* situation *abuse*,
And call them vile rascals with nothing to lose.
    Sing Ca Ira, Ca Ira, ah! ah!
      Ca Ira, Ca Ira, ah! ah!
    No insolent tyrants for me!

Thus the footpad who prowls thro' the night for his prey,
And takes the poor passenger's money away,
Then leaves him in *huff*, may be just as alert,
And I swear he's a beggar without any shirt.
    Sing Ca Ira, Ca Ira, ah! ah!
      Ca Ira, Ca Ira, ah! ah!
    The French revolution for me!

O ye, who are fond to be nicknam'd my lord;
And swagger in courts with a star and a sword!
Ye derive all your joy from ridiculous things,
The sycophant's bow, and the " *what, what*" of kings.
    Sing Ca Ira, Ca Ira, ah! ah!
      Ca Ira, Ca Ira, ah! ah!
    No childish damn'd nonsense for me!

Ye say, those who wish equal laws for mankind,
Are *Levelling reptiles*, presumptuous and blind;
But *you* are the *Levelling Race* we maintain,
For tho' character's *lost*, yet your titles *remain*.
    Sing Ca Ira, Ca Ira, ah! ah!
      Ca Ira, Ca Ira, ah! ah!
    No titles unmeaning for me!

Tho' the son of a peer be a rogue and a slave,
That son must *succeed*, when his sire's in the grave;
And the wise and the foolish, the bold and the base,
By turns be call'd majesty, highness, and grace.
    Sing Ca Ira, Ca Ira, ah! ah!
      Ca Ira, Ca Ira, ah! ah!
    No such levelling system for me!

That society must have distinction, we know,
But the good should be *high*, and the bad should be *low*;

'Tis virtue, or vice, wheresoever they're seen,
Makes a duke or a dustman, a drab or a queen.
  Sing Ca Ira, Ca Ira, ah! ah!
   Ca Ira, Ca Ira, ah! ah!
  All proper distinction for me!

When proud aristocracy pleads in behalf
Of court-chosen bishops, and judges, we laugh;
For bishops ne'er preach, and the judges—alas!
But truth is a libel, and so let it pass.
  Sing Ca Ira, Ca Ira, ah! ah!
   Ca Ira, Ca Ira, ah! ah!
  No court-chosen creatures for me.

Those must be tyrannical monsters we swear,
Who value *man* less than a partridge or hare;
Who, dead to all sympathy, lost to all shame,
Can imprison a wretch for the sake of *their game.*
  Sing Ca Ira, Ca Ira, ah! ah!
   Ca Ira, Ca Ira, ah! ah!
  No tyrannical monsters for me!

The people of Britain will ne'er be contented,
Until they are fairly, and well represented;
For as things go at present, no mercy they find,
And pow'r that's usurp'd is the scourge of mankind.
  Sing Ca Ira, Ca Ira, ah! ah!
   Ca Ira, Ca Ira, ah! ah!
  No vile usurpation for me!

Yet *Burke* the apostate, *Will Pitt,* and his crew,
Who have only their private advantage in view;
Without *blushing,* or mincing the matter, declare,
We shall have no redress, but remain as we are.
  Sing Ca Ira, Ca Ira, ah! ah!
   Ca Ira, Ca Ira, ah! ah!
  No selfish apostate for me!

The minister said in *his* house, that the nation
Possess'd at this time a *fair representation;*
But while *Borough mongers* and *Placemen* we spy,
We know very well that he told a damn'd lie.
   Sing Ca Ira, Ca Ira, ah! ah!
    Ca Ira, Ca Ira, ah! ah!
   No such representation for me!

Then let honest Britons adhere to the plan
Of reason, of truth, and the just rights of man;
Let us join hearts and hand to support the French
  nation,
Who fight for the world, and the world's reforma-
  tion.
   Sing Ca Ira, Ca Ira, ah! ah!
    Ca Ira, Ca Ira, ah! ah!
   Truth, justice, and freedom for me!

The BATTLE of MONMOUTH.

WHILST in peaceful quarter's lying,
  We indulge the glass too late:
Far remote the thoughts of dying,
  Hear, my friends, the soldier's fate:
From the summer's sun hot gleaming,
  Where the dusty clouds arise,
To the plains, where heroes screaming,
  Shouts and dying groans arise.
    SPOKEN.
Halt! halt! form every rank there,
  Mark yon dust that climbs the sky,
To the front, close up the rear!
  See the enemy is nigh.
Platoons, move to proper distance,
  Cover close each rank and file;
They will make a bold resistance,
  Here, my lads, is gallant toil.

Now all you from downy slumber,
    Rouse to softer joys of love,
Wake to pleasures without number,
    Peace and care your bosom prove.
Round us roars bellowing thunder,
    Ah! how close the iron storm;
To the fields, where pale ghosts wander :—
    Pass the word—form there, lads, form.

SPOKEN.

To the left, display the columns!
    Halt front, dress, be bold and brave;
Mark in the air a fiery column,
    Who'd refuse a glorious grave.
Open your boxes, quick be ready,
    See our light troops gain the hill;
Courage, lads, be firm and steady,
    Hence each care and fear be still.

Now half choak'd with dust and powder,
    Fiercely throbs each burning vein;
Hark! the din of arms now clashing,
    Ah! what heaps of heroes slain!
See the souls of brave men dying,
    Call for vengeance as they die;
Frowning still the dead, dying,
    Seem to threaten as they lie.

SPOKEN.

Bravely done, each gallant soldier,
    Well sustain'd that heavy fire;
Alexander ne'er was bolder,
    Now, by regiments, we'll retire;
See our second line move on us,
    Open your columns, give them way,
Heaven perhaps may smile upon us;
    These may yet regain the day.

See our second line engaging,
    Charging close, spread carnage round;
Fierce revenge, with fury raging,
    Angry heroes beat the ground:
See from flank to flank red flashing,
    How each volley rends the gloom:
Shout, huzza! what gallant clashing!
    Man and horse now meet their doom.

SPOKEN.

To the left oblikely firing,
    Let's be steady, level well,
Who wou'd think of e'er retiring,
    Here, my lads these volleys fell.
Hark, by heavens! dragoons flying!
    How each squadron fills the plain!
Check them, boys, you fear not dying!
    Sell yourselves, nor fall in vain.

Now our left wing they are turning,
    Carnage is but just begun;
Desp'rate now, it's useless mourning,
    Farewell friends, adieu each one:
Fix'd to die, we scorn retreating,
    To the shock our breasts oppose,
Hark, the sound! the signal's beating,
    See with bayonets they close.

SPOKEN.

Front, march!—Rear, make ready!—
    Forward, march! reserve your fire.
Now take aim, fire brisk, be steady,
    March, march, see their files retire;
On their left our light troops dashing,
    Now our dragoons charge their rear.
Shout, huzza! what gallant clashing;
    They run they run, hence banish, fear.

Now the toil and danger's over,
  Drefs alike each wounded brave;
Hope again infpires the lover,
  Old and young forget their grave;
Seize the canteen, poize it higher,
  Reft to each brave foul that fell;
Death for this is ne'er the nigher,
  Welcome mirth, and fear farewell.

The THIRSTING LOVER.

MY temples with clufters of grapes I'll entwin
  And barter all joys for a goblet of wine;
In fearch of a *Venus* no longer I'll run,
But ftop and forget her at *Bacchus's* tun.

Yet why this refolve to relinquifh the fair?
'Tis a folly for fpirits like mine to defpair;
For what mighty charms can be found in a glafs,
If not fill'd to the health of fome favourite lafs?

'Tis women whofe charms ev'ry rapture impart,
And lend a new fpring to the charms of the heart:
The mifer himfelf (fo fupreme is her fway)
Grows a convert to love, and returns her the key.

At the found of her voice, forrow lifts up her head,
And poverty liftens, quite pleas'd from her fhade;
While age, in an extacy, hobling along,
Beats time with her crutch, at the tune of her fong.

Then bring me a goblet from Bacchus's hoard,
The largeft and deepeft that ftands on the board;
I'll fill up a brimmer, and drink to the fair,
'Tis the toaft of a lover, and pledge me who dare?

L

The HERMIT.
By Mr. BEATTIE.

AT the close of the day, when the Hamlet is still,
  And mortals the sweets of forgetfulness prove,
When nought but the horrors is heard on the hill,
  And nought but the nightingale's song in the grove:
'Twas thus by a cave of a mountain afar,
  While his harp rung symphonious, a hermit began,
No more with himself, or with nature at war,
  He thought as a sage, tho' he felt as a man.

Ah why, all abandoned to darkness and woe,
  Why alone, Philomela, that languishing fall?
For spring shall return, and a lover bestow,
  And sorrow no longer thy bosom enthral.
But if pity inspire thee, renew the sad lay,
  Mourn, sweetest complainer, man calls thee to mourn,
O soothe him, whose pleasures like them nap away,
  Full quickly they pass—but they never return.

Now gliding remote, on the verge of the sky,
  The moon half extinguish'd, her crescent displays:
But lately I mark'd, while majestic on high,
  She shone, and the planets were lost in the blaze.
Roll on, thou fair orb, and with gladness pursue,
  The path that conducts thee to splendor again;
But man's faded glory, whose change shall renew,
  Ah fool! to exult in a glory so vain!

'Tis night, and the landscape is lovely no more;
  I mourn, but ye woodlands I mourn not for you,
For morn is returning your charms to restore,
  Perfum'd with fresh fragrance, and glittering with dew.

Nor yet for the ravage of winter I mourn,
   Kind nature the embrio blossom will save;
But when shall spring visit the mouldering urn?
   O when shall it dawn on the night of the grove!

The WINE VAULT.

Tune—The Hounds are all out.

By G. A. STEVENS.

CONTENTED I am, and contented I'll be,
   For what can this world more afford,
Than a girl that will sociably sit on my knee,
   And a cellar that's plentiful stor'd,
              My brave boys.

My vault-door is open, descend ev'ry guest,
   Broach that cask, aye, that wine we will try,
'Tis as sweet as the lips of your love to the taste,
   And as bright as her cheek to the eye.

In a piece of slit hoop, I my candle have stuck,
   'Twill light us each bottle to hand;
And the foot of my glass for the purpose I broke,
   For I hate that a bumper should stand.

We are dry where we sit, tho' the oozy drops seem
   The moist walls with wet pearls to emboss,
From the arch, moldy cobwebs in Gothic taste
    stream,
   Like stucco-work cut out of moss.

Astride on a butt, as a butt should be strode,
   I sit my companions among,
Like grape-blessing Bacchus, the good fellow's god,
   And a sentiment give, or a song.

I charge spoil in hand, and my empire maintain,
  No ancient more patriotic-like bled;
Each drop in defence of delight I will drain,
  And myself for my bucks I'll drink dead.

Sound that pipe, 'tis in tune, and those bins are well fill'd,
  View that heap of old hock in the rear,
Yon bottles of Burgundy, see how they're fill'd,
  Like artillery, tier over tier.

My cellar's my camp, and my soldiers my flasks,
  All gloriously rang'd in review;
When I cast my eyes round, I confider my casks,
  As kingdoms I've yet to subdue.

Like Macedon's madman, my drink I'll enjoy,
  In defiance of gravel and gout;
Who cry'd when he had no more worlds to subdue,
  I'll weep when my liquor is out.

When the lamp is brim full, see the flame brightly shines,
  But when wanting moisture, decays;
Replenish the lamp of my life with rich wines,
  Or else there's an end of my blaze.

'Tis my will when I die, not a tear should be shed,
  No *hic jacet* be cut on my stone;
But pour on my coffin a bottle of red,
  And say, *a choice fellow is gone.*
            My brave boys.

CORYDON and PHILLIS.
A Pastoral.

HER sheep had in clusters crept close to a grove,
  To hide from the heat of the day;
And Phillis herself in a wood'bine alcove,
  Among the sweet violets lay:

A young lamkin, it seems, had been stole from her
    dam,
  'Twixt Cupid and Hymen a plot,
That Corydon might, as he search'd for his lamb,
  Arrive at the critical spot.
As thro' the green hedge for his lamkin he peeps
  He saw the fair nymph with surprise;
Ye gods, if so killing, he cry'd while she sleeps,
  I'm lost, if she opens her eyes.
To tarry much longer would hazard my heart,
  I'll homeward my lamkin to trace;
But in vain honest Corydon strove to depart,
  For love held him fast to the place.

Cease, cease, pretty birds, what a chirping you keep,
  I think you too loud on the spray;
Don't you see, foolish lark, that the charmer's
    asleep,
  You'll wake her as sure as 'tis day:
How dare that fond butterfly touch the sweet maid,
  Her cheeks he mistakes for the rose;
I'd put him to death, if I were not afraid
  My boldness would break her repose.

Then Phillis look'd up with a languishing smile,
  Kind shepherd, says she, you mistake,
I laid myself down for to rest me awhile,
  But trust me, I've long been awake:
The shepherd took courage, advanc'd with a bow,
  He plac'd himself down by her side;
And manag'd the matter, I cannot tell how,
  But yesterday made her his bride.

FRIENDSHIP.—A SONG.

FRIENDSHIP to every willing mind,
  Opens a heavenly treasure;
There may the sons of sorrow find,
  Sources of real pleasure:

See what employments men pursue,
  Then you will own my words are true;
Friendship alone unfolds to view
  Sources of real pleasure.

Poor are the joys which fools esteem,
  Fading and transitory;
Mirth is as fleeting as a dream,
  Or a delusive story:
Luxury leaves a sting behind,
  Wounding the body and the mind;
Only in Friendship can we find,
  Pleasure and solid glory.

Beauty, with all its gaudy shows,
  Is but a painted bubble;
Short is the triumph, wit bestows,
  Full of deceit and trouble:
Fame, like a shadow, flees away,
  Titles and dignities decay;
Nothing but friendship can display
  Joys that are free from trouble.

Learning, that boasted glitt'ring thing,
  Scarcely is worth possessing;
Riches forever on the wing,
  Cannot be call'd a blessing:
Sensual pleasures swell desire,
  Just as the fuel feeds the fire;
Friendship can real bliss inspire,
  Bliss, that is worth possessing.

Happy the man who has a friend,
  Form'd by the God of nature;
Well may he feel and recommend
  Friendship, for his Creator:
Then as our hearts in friendship join,
  So let our social power combine;
Rul'd by a passion most divine,
  Friendship with our Creator.

COLUMBIAN SONGSTER.

SONG.

Tune—God Save, &c.

GOD save—"THE RIGHTS OF MAN!"
Give him a heart to scan
    Blessings so dear;
Let them be spread around,
Wherever man is found,
And with the welcome sound,
    Ravish his ear!

See from the universe,
Darkness and clouds disperse;
    Mankind awake!
Reason and truth appear,
Freedom advances near,
Monarchs with terror hear.
    See how they quake!

Sore have we felt the stroke;
Long have we bore the yoke,
    Sluggish and tame;
But now the lion roars,
And a loud note he pours;
Spreading to distant shores,
    LIBERTY's flame.

Let us with France agree,
And bid *the World be free*—
    Leading the way.
Let tyrants all conspire,
Fearless of sword and fire,
FREEDOM shall ne'er retire;
    FREEDOM shall sway!

Godlike, and great the strife,
Life will indeed be life,
    Should we prevail.

Death, is so just a cause,
Crown us with loud applause,
And from tyrannic laws.
    Bid us—ALL HAIL!

O'er the Germanic pow'rs,
Big indignation low'rs,
    Ready to fall!
Let the rude savage host,
In their long numbers boast,
FREEDOM's almighty trust,
    Laughs at them all.

[FAME! Let thy trumpet sound!
Tell all the world around!
    Tell each degree!
Tell ribands, crowns, and zars,
Kings, traitors, troops, and wars,
Plans, councils, plots, and jars,
    FRENCHMEN ARE FREE.]

God save—"THE RIGHTS OF MAN!"
Give him a heart to scan
    Blessings so dear!
Let them be spread around,
Wherever man is found,
And with the welcome sound,
    Ravish his ear!

HAIL! HAPPY AMERICANS!

COLUMBIA! Columbia! to glory arise,
  The queen of the world, and the child of the skies;
Thy genius commands thee, with raptures behold,
While ages on ages thy splendors unfold:

Thy reign is the laſt, and the nobleſt of time,
Moſt fruitful thy ſoil, moſt inviting thy clime;
Let the climes of the eaſt ne'er incrimſon thy name,
Be freedom, and ſcience, and virtue thy fame.

To conqueſt and ſlaughter, let Europe aſpire,
Whelm nations in blood, wrap cities in fire;
Thy heroes the rights of mankind ſhall defend,
And triumph purſue them, and glory attend;
A world is thy realm, for a world be thy laws,
Enlarg'd as thy empire, and juſt as thy cauſe;
On freedom's broad baſis, that empire ſhall riſe,
Extend with the main, and diſſolve with the ſkies.

Fair ſcience her gate to thy ſons ſhall unbar,
And the eaſt ſee thy morn hide the beams of her ſtar;
New bards and new ages unrival'd ſhall ſoar,
To fame unextinguiſh'd, when time is no more:
To thee the laſt refuge of virtue's deſign'd,
Shall fly from all nations, the beſt of mankind;
There, grateful to Heaven, with tranſport ſhall bring,
Their incenſe more flagrant than odors of ſpring.

Nor leſs ſhall the fair ones to glory aſcend,
And genius and beauty in harmony blend;
The graces of form ſhall awake pure deſire,
And the charms of the ſoul ſtill enliven the fire:
Their ſweetneſs unmingled, their manners refin'd,
And virtue's bright image in ſtamp'd on the mind;
With peace and ſweet rapture ſhall teach life to glow,
And light up a ſmile in the aſpect of woe.

Thy fleets to all regions thy power ſhall diſplay,
The nations admire, and the ocean obey;
Each ſhore to thy glory its tribute unfold,
And the eaſt and the ſouth yield their ſpices and gold;

As the day spring unbounded thy splendors shall
    flow,
And earth's little kingdoms before thee shall bow;
While the ensigns of union in triumph unfurl'd,
Hush anarchy's sway, and give peace to the world.

Thus as down a lone valley with cedars o'erspread,
From the noise of the town I pensively stray'd,
The gloom from the face of fair Heaven retir'd,
The winds ceas'd to murmur, the thunders expir'd;
Perfumes as of Eden, flow'd sweetly along,
And a voice, as of angels, enchantingly sung,
Columbia! Columbia! to glory arise,
The queen of the world, and the child of the skies.

―――

The NORTHERN HUNT,
Or, BRUNSWICK's BEAGLES.
A NEW SONG.

THE Nimrods of the North had among them-
    selves agreed, sir!
To let all their blood hounds loose, and make Gal-
    lic Freedom bleed, sir!
A huntsman bold, call'd Brunswick, was leader of
    the pack, sir!
Who vow'd by all the Gods, to lay Freedom on
    her back, sir!
        Bow, wow, wow, &c.

His whippers-in were Clairfayt, Coubire, and Ho-
    henloe, sir!
With Broglio and Conde—a fierce and fiery crew,
    sir!
His dogs were staunch and numerous, occustom'd
    to the chace, sir!
And furious to hunt Freedom down, if they could
    but her trace, sir!
        Bow, wow, wow, &c.

Poor Freedom look'd around her, and faw, with
    confternation,
No friendly neighbour near her, to 'fend her from
    proftration:
In vain fhe look'd to England, in vain fhe look'd
    to Spain, fir!
In vain fhe look'd to Switzerland, to Holland look'd
    in vain, fir!
   Bow, wow, wow, &c.

Diftrefs'd, to Heav'n fhe cry'd, fir!—Kind Heav'n
    was pleas'd to hear her;
And rous'd her Gauls to guard her life from dangers
    now fo near her:
Three hundred thoufand arms at once were rais'd
    to 'venge her caufe, fir!
And fnatch her from the yawning gapes of Bruns-
    wick's beagles jaws, fir!
   Bow, wow, wow, &c.

Mean while the Bully buccaneer, advanc'd with
    hue and cry, fir!
And fwore, that all who took the part, of Liberty,
    fhould die, fir!
His curs, innur'd to flaughter, fet up a hedious yell,
    fir!
They feem'd the whelps of Cerberus, on purpofe
    fent from Hell, fir!
   Bow, wow, wow, &c.

Their yelps were heard at Longwy, their yelps were
    heard at Verdun,
Where traitors daftardly exclaim'd, Helas! nous
    voici perdus!
They threw themfelves at Brunfwick's feet, and
    begg'd their lives he'd fpare, fir!
Ignoble deed!—But woe's my heart! No friend had
    Freedom there, fir!
   Bow, wow, wow, &c.

Not so at Thionville and Lisle (immortal names in story)
True Frenchmen here his threats defy, and pant for civic glory!
In vain Saxe Teschen's dogs—and bitches—bark around the burning trenches!
A hero, here, is ev'ry boy; a heroine, ev'ry wench is!
      Bow, wow, wow, &c.

Not long these barkings shall ye hear, illustrious men of Flanders!
For, lo! Dumourier comes apace, with other brave commanders;
Already have the Prussian packs retreated in disorder,
With marks of shame upon their backs, from all the Gallic border!
      Bow, wow, wow, &c.

Wait but a week, and persevere, your city in defending;
Nor doubt to see, of all your woes, a speedy, happy ending:
Soon shall the puny Roman King be forc'd, like old Porsenna,
To call his blood hounds back again to kennel at Vienna!
      Bow, wow, wow, &c.

With scourge in hand, pursue the route of those invading ranters;
And free, from Austria's galling yoke, the long enslav'd Brabanters.
So shall the Nimrods of the North be taught more moderation,
And ne'er again let loose their hounds at any freeborn nation.
      Bow, wow, wow, &c.

ON the cliffs of the *Andes*, where virtue once reign'd,
    The voice of true freedom is heard;
There tyranny long has her empire sustain'd,
    Over plains, where once worth was rever'd.

But tyranny soon may lament the sad yoke,
    Which over these regions he cast;
His sceptre is shatter'd, his courage quite broke;
    And at freedom now trembles at last.

The beams of humanity mildly have shone,
    O'er countries which droop'd under rage;
They own the mild warmth of our more northern sun,
    And dare in all conflicts engage.

Our states the first glorious example display'd,
    Which soon ov'r the world shall be spread;
All shall share in our freedom, and shall share in our trade,
    Whilst Columbians on tyranny tread.

But here let me mention, whilst tears stain each cheek,
    The fate of the Spanish bold chief:
A new world determin'd o'er ocean to seek,
    He wish'd to the natives relief.

His valor was great, and his conduct renown'd;
    Humanity still was his aim;
Three ages the worth of *Columbus* resound,
    By virtue aspiring to fame,

Both Spaniards and natives still wishing to bless,
  Worth and commerce he still kept in view;
He thought—but the victim, alas! of distress,
  Vile rancour he could not subdue.

Behold him at length, quite bereft of support,
  In chains, in a dungeon confin'd;
The martyr he died of a barbarous court;
  But a moral has left for mankind.

On ev'ry heart be that moral impress'd,
  Ye patriots! ye heroes! attend;
And learn, that a courtier good faith ne'er express'd,
  That a king can be never a friend.

Belisarius, if ever *Justinian* could slight,
  True reason such rule must disown;
And all should the praise of Columbus recite,
  Whilst Philip disgrac'd a great throne.

Richmond, October 12, 1792.

COUPLETS pour la fête de la CONSTITUTION,
  acceptée par le Roi des FRANCAIS.

AUJOURD'HUY que l'egalité
  Détruit la tyrannie,
Amis, fêtons la liberté,
  En depit de l'envie;
    Par de vifs transports,
    Joignons nos accords.
Avec ceux de la France;
    Douce liberté,
    Sous la déité,
D'un peuple qui t'encense.

Laisse, aristocrate orgueillieux,
  Les titres de ton père,
Crois moi, tous les titres pompeux,
  Ne sont qu'une chimère;
    Ces papiers moisis,
    Objets de mépris,
Font-ils donc plus de gloire
    Qu'un simple laurier,
    Que cueile un guerier
Aux champs de la victoire.

Ah! Si par quelqu' événement
  La France se divise,
Ou vaincre, ou mourir promptement,
  Voila notre devise;
    Fidèle à la loi,
    La nation, le roi,
Qu'au sein de l'allegresse
    Chaqu'un à present,
    Fasse le ferment
De tenir sa promesse.

Grand Washington, plus qu'aucun roi
  L'Europe te révére;
Chaque Americain voit en toi
  Un citoyen, un frere;
    Tous ces conquirants
    N'étoient que tyrants
Faits pour troubler la terre;
    Généréux vainqueur,
    A louer ta valeur
Tu force l'Angleterre.

La desse que nous fêtons
  Voit en ces liedieux son temple;
Messieurs, instruits par vos leçons,
  Nous suivons votre exemple:
    Le verre à la main,
    Chantons ce refrain,

Qu'une double alliance,
    Par des nœuds facrés,
    Unisse à jamais
L.'Amerique et la France.

Citoyens de divers pays,
    Préfents à cette fête;
Vous qui vous êtes réunis
    Pour la rendre complette ;
    A nos envieux,
    Dites en tous lieux,
Que des deux hémifpheres,
    Par de vifs tranfports,
    Joignant leurs accords,
Vous avez vu des frères.

SONG.

For the Glorious Fourteenth of July.

Air—To Anacreon in Heaven.

THE genius of France from his ftar begem'd throne,
O'r his valorous fons bent his foftering eye,
Under wars fanguine power not long fhall ye groan,
    Fair freedom he cries fmiling fhoots from the fky.
    Your caufe on the records of Heaven is plac'd ;
    Defpots and crowns fhall from earth be erac'd;
While the Sun more refulgent fhall dart his bright ray,
To cheer and illumine this glorious day.

With baftiles my lov'd land fhall no more be difgrac'd,
    Her white banners around ye, humanity waves :

No more shall the image of God be defac'd,
  Or dark cells be contriv'd by cruelty's slaves:
    The deep groan of anguish is now heard no
      more;
    Your whips and your tortures ye tyrants are
      o'er,
And soon shall the world in unison say,
Forever be bless'd this glorious day.

The bright star of liberty arose in the North,*
  O'er the Atlantic's rough wave her splendors she
    shed;
For justice and virtue soon hurried her forth,
  O'er thy realms my lov'd Gallia her influence
    spread,
    And oh may her power your spirits inspire!
    And still may you glow with her sacred fire;
While each son of Freedom exulting shall say,
Forever be bless'd this glorious day.

Let the valor of Washington live in each heart,
  And those chiefs who for liberty drain'd ev'ry
    vein,
While honor'd, their spirits flown above are at rest,
  Their memory unfading forever shall reign;
    Like their's be your fame undaunted and free,
    Firmly rooted the basis of freedom shall be;
Her favors around ye brightly shall play,
Adding new glory to this happy day.

Thy cause, struggling France, is the cause of the
    world;
  His tyranny over millions shall one man extend!
From their thrones be these ministers by liberty
    hurl'd,
  And each man to each prove protector and friend.
    The æra arrives, already 'tis near,
    When this sound alone shall be brought to the
      ear:

* *North-America.*

May freedom and friendship emit a joint ray,
To gild and adorn this glorious day.
   New-York, July 17, 1793.

Occasional ODE *for the* 17*th of June,* 1776.

NOW let rich music sound,
   And all the regions round
      With rapture fill;
Let the full trump of fame
To Heaven itself proclaim
The everlasting name
      Of Bunker's Hill.

Beneath this sky-wrapt brow
What heroes sleep below;
      How dear to Jove!
Not more belov'd were those
Who foil'd celestial foes,
When the old giants rose
      To arms above.

Now scarce eleven short years
Have roll'd their rapid spheres,
      Through Heaven's high road!
Since o'er yon swelling tide
Pass'd all the British pride,
And water'd Bunker's side
      With foreign blood.

Then Charlestown's gilded spires
Felt unrelenting fires,
      And sunk in night;
But, Phœnix like, they'll rise
From where their ruin lies,
And strike the astonish'd eyes
      With glories bright.

Meand'ring to the deep,
Majestic Charles* shall weep
      Of war no more;
Fam'd as the Appian Way,
The world's first Bridge, to day,
All nations shall convey
      From shore to shore.

On our bless'd Mountain's head
The festive board we'll spread
      With viands high;
Let joy's broad bowls go round,
With public spirit crown'd,
We'll consecrate the ground
      To LIBERTY.

* *Charles River, Boston,* 1776.

CIVIC SONG.

The NEW "DAUPHIN" *to the tune of the old.*

ALL hail! to Freedom's Sons,
    Who arms and arts combine,
Whose brows the Laurel-crown,
    And Olive wreath intwine!
No perjur'd Monarch's first-born son,
    Inspires our festive voice;
A nation's natal day commands
    Columbia to rejoice!

CHORUS.

Let Fame her loudest Clarion sound,
    To celebrate the birth
Of Freedom, child of Heaven,
    And Dauphin of the earth.

No more the scepter'd knave,
    Nor vile assassin crown'd,
A subject world shall sway,
    And by that world renown'd.

For equal, free-born man no more
　　Will bear a tyrant's chains,
Because the blood of ages flows
　　In his polluted veins.
　　　　　Cho. *Let Fame, &c.*

Borne on the swiftest wings,
　　That plume the flight of time,
Her flambeau Freedom flings,
　　And kindles every clime;
The fire of truth, which Bourbon's throne,
　　With vollied flames o'er ran;
Now spreads o'er earth the electric shock,
　　And nerves the slave to man.
　　　　　Cho. *Let Fame, &c.*

May that fair sun whose beams
　　First ray'd Columbia's shore,
Each distant zone illume,
　　And rise to set no more.
And now, by deathless heroes rear'd,
　　Behold a temple rise,
Whose base on Nature's rock is laid,
　　Whose roof shall touch the skies!
　　　　　Cho. *Let Fame, &c.*

Philadelphia, 1793.

ODE *for the* CIVIC FEAST.
By a Citizen of Boston.

AGAIN by the spirit of Freedom invited,
Round her fire we convene to rejoice in its rays;
　Th' ethereal flame, in America lighted,
Throughout regions far distant burst forth in a blaze.
　　CHORUS.—Frenchmen are free!
　　　　　Our good allies
　　　　　Know how to prize
　　" *The Rights of Man*" and Liberty.

The fluid electric through ether suspended,
In a torrent of light'ning surrounds our abode;
So *Freedom's pure fire* has from Heav'n descended,
And requires but a *Franklin* to manage the rod.

Chorus.—*Frenchmen are free, &c.*

GRAND CHORUS.

Crowns and sceptres yield their pow'r;
Princely honors fade away;
Despots will be known no more!
Reason now assumes her sway.

In France *true Patriots*, as a *Franklin*, are guiding,
O'er the heads of the foes of *Just Rights* the full stroke;
The storms which preceded the shock are subsiding,
And the clouds which o'erhung, are dispersing in smoke.

Chorus.—*Frenchmen are free, &c.*

Sad regions of sorrow *this flame* shall enlighten:
Where the *groans* of *distress* compose *music* for *kings*,
Shall Liberty's rays the whole Atmosphere brighten,
And the blessings abound, which Equality brings.

Chorus.—*Frenchmen are free, &c.*

GRAND CHORUS.

Crowns and sceptres yield their pow'r;
Princely honors fade away;
Despots will be known no more!
Reason now assumes her sway.

PADDY's FAREWELL;

Or, An Irish Account of French Affairs.

Tune—When I was a young Man in sweet Tipparary.

DON'T blubber, dear Norah, I beg you'd be easy,
    For soon will you see your fond Paddy again,
Returning with laurels, with liberty crazy,
    An eye or two less, or a limb or two lame.

CHORUS.

Sing ditheru, how d'ye do, Patrick Shelalay,
    To the right about, fight it out, all the day long;
Cut and flash, Frenchmen hash, pop away gaily,
    Suck away, while you may, whisky so strong!

I'm going to beat all the Frenchmen, my jewel,
    Because they presume to make laws of their own;
They want all men *equal*—that would be dam'd cruel,
    For then each great monarch must jump from his throne.   Sing ditheru, &c.

Then what do you think of their roguish convention?
    They plunder'd their bishops because they were *poor*;
Depriv'd ev'ry knave of his title and pension,
    And turn'd all the Nuns and the Monks out of door.   Sing ditheru, &c.

And then they've abolish'd *belief* in *damnation*,
    To save the expence of a priest or a church;
For now, I am told, *Sans Culottes* congregation
    Have left popes and crosiers and beads in the lurch.   Sing ditheru, &c.

That priests have come over to live by subscription,
　No doubt its much better than feeding on frogs;
I'd make them a gift of a fitter description,
　By subscribing—a halter a piece to the dogs.
　　　　　　Sing ditheru, &c.

Of treason they think that a king can be guilty!
　Their own they condemn'd for not keeping his word;
They say to their subjects, all kings should swear fealty,
Not their subjects to them—och monstrous absurd!
　　　　　　Sing ditheru, &c.

And as (what exceeds all their former transgressions)
　They've trampled on king craft, and pull'd down her throne;
Let's unite with the Austrians, Prussians, and Hessians,
As we're without sin, let us cast the first stone!
　　　　　　Sing ditheru, &c.

O D E

For SAINT TAMMANY's DAY, May 1, 1785.

(Written by Teuxogrondi, a Delaware Chief.)

DONNA makoo makoonas!
　Kuskoo donna makoo:
Wawa nekoonos!
Gwahee honigee.
　　Full Chorus.
Ever sacred be this day,
Genial morn of rosy May.

Recitative.

To Schuylkill's fair banks let us chearful repair,
For pure is the æther, and fragrant the air;
Soft Zephyrs shall fan us, and eke thro' the grove,
The genius of *Tammany* shield us with love.
No foes shall intrude with inquisitive eye,
Our orgies, our dances, or myst'ries to spy.

Air.

Adieu to your wives,
Come gird on your knives,
   Your tamahawks, arrows, and bows!
Your bodies besmear,
With oil of the bear,
   And look undismay'd on your foes.

Recitative.

Kindle up the council fires,
Lo! our Saint the flame inspires;
Whilst we pass the flowing bowl,
Let the smoaky volumes roll,
From the calimut and pipe,
Of sweet Peace the welcome type.
Let our Sachems healths go round,
Beat with nimble foot the ground:
'Till the woods and hills reply,
Vocal mirth and symphony.

Chorus.

Ever sacred be this day,
Genial morn of rosy May.

Recitative.

Now the Hatchet we'll bury, since War is no more,
And Peace with rich plenty revisits our shore;
To hunt the fleet Stag o'er the mountains we'll run,
In sports we alone will employ the fell gun.
Our fields shall be cloath'd with gay harvests again,
And friendship will brighten the blood-rusted chain:

But should war call us forth, then adieu to our glee,
Each shoulders his rifle, and takes to his tree.

Air.
Hail, Columbia's Tutelar!
Tho' thy ashes, distant are,
Hid beneath the mountain side,
Or below the rapid tide:
Still thy warlike shade attends,
Smiling on thy filial friends;
Leads their dances, aids their pleasure,
Joys dispensing, without measure.

Recitative.
Now each Sachem join hand round the Liberty Pole,
And briskly again, pass the heart-cheering bowl:
To Washington's mem'ry,—the chief of our train,
The full-flowing goblet, repeated we'll drain:
Then next, to each Cheiftain who fought and who bled,
Let's sing a Requiem, and toast him, tho' dead.

Air.
For Tammany, holy,
Let's fire a volley,
   That hills, woods and rocks may reply;
We'll found him in powder,
Still louder and louder,
'Till echo shall rend the blue sky.

Chorus.
Ever sacred be this day,
Genial morn of rosy May.

Recitative.
In volumes of smoke, and in spires of flame,
   Our Tutelar flew to the Spheres;
He left us his blessing, his weapons, his fame,
   And hearts unacquainted with fears.
The shades of our ancestors cluster'd around,
   To welcome our Chief from the wars;
With laurels celestial his temples they bound,
   Then thron'd him on high 'midst the stars,

N

Air.

Sound the horns, ye tuneful choirs,
'Tis our Saint, the notes inspires;
Brace the drums, and make them roll,
Martial Music charms the soul:
Soon, responsive to the chorus,
Tammany shall stand before us,
On the mossy, velvet green,
Smiling on us, tho' unseen.

Chorus.

Charge the bowl again with liquor,
Pass it briskly, push it quicker;
Sachems, Warriors, now advance,
Form the ring, begin the dance!
Music summons us to pleasure,
Mark the tune, and time the measure:
Full of mirth, and full of glee,
Thus concludes our Jubilee.

Grand Chorus.

Ever sacred be this day;
Genial morn of rosy May.

SONG.

AIR.—INDIAN CHIEF.

WHEN a nation's obsorb'd under Tyranny's chain,
Oppress'd by the mandates of monarchical reign,
As the tyrants arose, so the subjects sunk down,
And the centre of glory remain'd in a *crown*.

But a light breaking forth, sent by Heaven's decree,
And a voice from above, bids the nations be free;
AMERICA answers—" We're young and but small,"
Yet Great God of Nature, we rise at thy call.

Though short is our arm, yet a *banner* we'll raise,
Oppos'd to all tyrants, to freedom a praise:
A period the goddess demands us to fix—
It's the *Fourth of July*, in the year *Seventy-Six!*

Feats of glory we pass'd, too great to recount,
While our *Moses* extended his arm on the mount,
Extirpated the foe, and arose to bright fame;
And the nations of Europe are catching the flame.

Let Gallia's great name be remember'd this day,
While the ensigns of freedom with us they display;
A sound constitution our unity binds,
Since all *Arnold's* and *Dumourier's* are purg'd from
   our lines.

Let trumpets of joy, from the great *Belvedere*,
Reach to France, by its echo salute the glad air;
And the founder of this still belong to the choir,
Whom the spirit of freedom and zeal shall inspire.

The nations discover that freedom's the sole,
And their *Crowns* they'll exchange for a *Cap* or a
   Pole;
And a head to presumptuous a crown to support,
Will pass condemnation in Liberty's court.

Let bumpers be fill'd from that unfailing spring,
Toast all sons of earth, and drink Freedom—*No*
   King!
'Till time shall be swallowed in unfading day,
For *Freedom* and *Peace* we'll occasionally pray.

 Belvidere Club-House, N. York, July 4, 1793.

SONG.

WHILE tyranny marshals her minions around,
 And bid her fierce legions advance,
Fair freedom, the hopes of thy sons to confound,
 To restore her old empire in France.

What friend among men, to the Rights of Mankind,
  But is fir'd with resentment to see,
The Satraps of pride and oppression combin'd
  To prevent a great land's being free.

Europe's fate on the contest's decision depends,
  Most important its issue will be;
For should France be subdu'd, Europe's liberty ends,
  If she triumphs, the world will be free.

Then let every true patriot unite in her cause,
  A cause of such moment to man—
Let all whose souls spurn at tyrannical laws,
  Lend her all the assistance they can.

May the spirit of Sparta her armies inspire,
  And the star of America guide;
May a Washington's wisdom, a Hamilton's fire,
  In her camps and her councils preside.

May her sons fatal discord no longer divide,
  'Mong her chiefs may no Arnold's be found,
But may they united, resist the rough tide,
  'Till their toils be with victory crown'd.

And at length, when sweet peace from her sphere
    shall descend—
  When the fiends of oppression have fled,
Immortal renown, shall those heroes attend,
  Who for freedom, fought, conquer'd and bled.

Blazon'd high, then their deeds shall swell history's
    page,
  And adorn lofty poetry's lays;
While the mem'ry of tyrants, the cause of their age,
  In oblivion's dark bastile decays.

The Patriots have oblig'd the proud Duke to retreat,
  And we dare to applaud the great deed;
We dare to exult in a tyrant's defeat,
  And rejoice that a nation is freed.

For this we assemble, despising all those
    Who wish to enslave the free mind;
France's foes we are conscious are liberty's foes,
    And her friends are the friends of mankind.

If angels e'er learn from the mansions above,
    The affairs of our planet to scan,
They could not this glorious event but approve,
    As the noblest exertion of man.

Patriots of each servile nation, arise,
    And enjoy what the Deity gave;
To be free is the duty man owes the All Wise,
    And he sins who is tamely a slave.

On the rock of Man's Rights France a fortress has plann'd,
    Which thro' many a bright age shall endure;
Like a crag 'midst the waves undisturb'd shall it stand,
    And preserve Heaven's blessings secure.

With electrical force thro' the nations around,
    Her fire may dear liberty dart;
'Mong the sons of the north may its glow soon be found,
    May it warm each American's heart.

Cross the huge snowy Alps, to a region once dear,
    May the soul lifting influence be hurl'd;
May its radiance the whole human family cheer,
    And may tyrants be banish'd the world.

New-Brunswick (N. J.) Jan. 1793.

MARY's DREAM.

THE moon had climb'd the highest hill
    That rises o'er the source of Dee,
And from the eastern summit shed
    Her silver light on tow'r and tree;

When Mary laid her down to sleep,
  Her thoughts on Sandy far at sea:
When soft and low a voice was heard
  Say—Mary, weep no more for me.

She from her pillow gently rais'd
  Her head to ask who there might be,
And saw young Sandy shivering stand,
  With palid cheek and hollow eye.
O, Mary dear! cold is my clay,
  It lies beneath a stormy sea;
Far, far from thee, I sleep in death,
  So, Mary, weep no more for me.

Three stormy nights and stormy days,
  We toss'd upon the raging main,
And long we strove our bark to save,
  But all our striving was in vain:
E'en then, when horror chill'd my blood,
  My heart was fill'd with love for thee;
The storm is past, and I at rest,
  So, Mary, weep no more for me.

O! Maiden dear, thyself prepare,
  We soon shall meet upon that shore,
Where love is free from doubt or care,
  And thou and I shall part no more.
Loud crow'd the cock! the shadow fled!
  No more of Sandy could she see;
But soft the passing spirit said,
  O! Mary! weep no more for me.

WHILE HIGH THE FOAMING SURGES RISE.

WHILE high the foaming surges rise,
  And pointed rocks appear,
Loud thunders rattle in the skies,
  Yet sailors must not fear.
    In storms, in wind,
    Their duty mind;

Aloft, below,
    They cheerful go,
To reef or steer, as 'tis design'd,
No fear or dangers fill the mind.

The signal for the line is made,
    The haughty foe's in sight;
The bloody flag's aloft display'd,
    And fierce the dreadful fight.
        Each minds his gun,
        No dangers shun;
        Aloft, below,
        They cheerful go,
Tho' thunders roar, yet still we find
No fears alarm the sailor's mind.

The storm is hush'd, the battle's o'er,
    The sky is clear again;
We tofs the cann to those on shore,
    While we are on the main.
        To Poll and Sue,
        Sincere and true;
        The grog goes round,
        With pleasure crown'd.
In war or peace, alike you'll find,
That honor fills the sailor's mind.

AN ODE,

On the adoption of the FEDERAL CONSTITUTION.

Tune—The Dauphin.

CROWN'D with auspicious light,
    Columbia's Eagle rise;
Thine emblems bless our sight,
    Thine honours greet our eyes.
Nations admire thy rising dawn,
    And shall salute thy day,
While generations yet unborn,
    Receive the genial ray.

CHORUS.

An empire's born, let cannon roar,
   Bid echo rend the sky;
Let every heart adore,
   High Heaven, our great ally.

Illustrious æra, hail—
   Thy stars in union grow,
Opposing mists dispell,
   And with fresh splendor glow.
Thy glories burst upon the gloom,
   Where darkness dragg'd her chain;
The sons of cruelty and death,
   Shall own thy gentle reign.
         Cho. *An Empire's born, &c.*

Let joy our hearts engage,
   Let foul contention cease;
Exchange for jealous rage,
   The enrapturing smile of peace.
No genius human e'er devis'd
   A federal plan more pure;
Wisdom and strength, and freedom guard,
   Columbia's rights secure.
         Cho. *An Empire's born, &c.*

Now Fame exert your powers.
   Your silver trumpet raise:
Still Washington is ours,
   Though earth proclaim his praise.
He once in crimson fields of blood,
   Forbade us to be slaves;
And now with an illustrious hand
   Again his country saves.
         Cho. *An Empire's born, &c.*

Discord aghast shall frown,
   Science her temple rear;
Labour ensure her crown,
   And useful arts appear.

Then bend your spears to pruning hoods,
  Break up the gen'rous soil,
While fruits of plenty round the land,
  Reward the reaper's toil.
      Cho. *An Empire's born, &c.*

Commerce your sails display,
  While agriculture sings:
Where late the bramble lay,
  The rose of beauty springs.
Union shall glad revolving years,
  No partial views remain;
Justice aloft advance her scale,
  And public virtue reign.
      Cho. *An Empire's born, &c.*

ON SLAVERY.
Tune—The Son of Alknomack, &c.

THE power that created the night and the day,
  Gave his image divine to each model of clay;
Tho' on different features, the God he imprest,
One spirit immortal pervades ev'ry breast.
    And Nature's great Charter the right never gave,
    That one mortal another should dare to enslave.

The same genial ray that the lillies unfold,
Gives the diamond its lustre, its brightness to gold—
That which Europe's proud sons to rapture inspire,
Warms each African breast with as genial a fire.
      And Nature's great Charter, &c.

May the head be corrected, subdu'd the proud soul,
That would fetter free limbs, and free spirits controul:
Be the gem or in ebon, or iv'ry enshrin'd,
The same form of heart, warms the whole human kind.
      And Nature's great Charter, &c.

May Freedom, whose rays we are taught to adore,
Beam bright as the sun, and bless every shore;
No Charter that pleads for the rights of mankind,
To invest these with gold, those with fetters can
　　bind.
　　And Nature's great Charter, the right never gave,
　That one mortal another should dare to enslave.

A NEW SONG.

Tune—Hark! hark! the joy inspiring Horn!

HARK! Hark! a joyous, cheering sound
Hails those, in chains monarch'al, bound;
　　Greets every Freeman's ear!
'Tis Freedom's voice! the glad'ning song
Bursts forth in raptures from her tongue,
　　Her Gallic cause to cheer!

My Sons, she cried, the day's your own,
And vict'ry all your toils shall crown;
　　Fell Monarchy must die!
In Europe's climes, no King shall reign;
But Liberty rule each domain
　　Supreme in majesty!

Columbia smiles! her joys encrease!
Her sons are bles'd with Plenty—Peace!
　　The fruits of Bravery!
Her heroes, boldly, took the field;
Determin'd, nobly, not to yield
　　To Kingly knavery!

From her example—Frenchmen, then,
Persist—Support your Rights as Men;
　　And bravely, whilst you can,
My Standard plant in Gallia's ground;
And *thunder* to the Nations round.
　　THE DIGNITY OF MAN!!!

THE MULBERRY TREE.
A NEW SONG.

THE sweet briar grows in the merry green
  wood,
 Where the musk-rose diffuses its perfume so free;
But the blight often siezes both blossom and bud;
 While the mildew flies over the *Mulberry Tree.*

In the nursery rear'd like the young tender vine,
 Mankind of all orders, and ev'ry degree,
First crawl on the ground, then spring up like the
  pine,
 And some branch and bear fruit, like the *Mulberry*
  Tree.

To the fair tree of knowledge some twine like a
  twig,
 While some sappy sprouts with their fruits disa-
  gree;
For which we from *birch* now and then pluck a
  twig,
 Which is not quite so sweet as the *Mulberry Tree.*

The vast tree of life we all eagerly climb,
 And impatiently pant at its hightop to be,
Tho' nine out of ten is lopp'd off in their prime,
 And they drop like dead leaves from the *Mulberry*
  Tree.

Some live by the *leaf*, and some live by the *bow*,
 As the *song*, or the *dance*, their vocation may be,
And some live and thrive, tho' we know no more
  how,
 Than the dew that flies over the *Mulberry Tree.*

But like weeping willows we hang down the head,
 When poor wither'd elders we're destin'd to be,
And we're minded no more than mere logs when
  we're dead,
 Or the dew that flies over the *Mulberry Tree.*

Yet like *lignum-vitæ* we hearts of oak wear,
  Or the *cedar* that keeps from the canker worm free,
While the vine-juice we drain to dissolve ev'ry care,
  Like the dew that flies over the *Mulberry Tree*.

ODE,

On the FOURTH of JULY.

COME all ye sons of song,
  Pour the full sound along,
    In joyful strains.
Beneath these western skies,
See a new empire rise,
Bursting with glad surprise,
    Tyrannic chains.

Liberty, with keen eye,
Pierc'd the blue vaulted sky,
    Resolv'd us free;
From her imperial seat,
Beheld the bleeding state,
Approv'd *this day's* debate,
    And firm decree.

Sublime, in awful form,
Amid the whirling storm,
    The Goddess stood:
She saw with pitying eye,
War's tempest raging high
Our heroes bravely die,
    In fields of blood.

High on his shining car,
Mars the stern god of war,
    Our struggle blest.

Soon vict'ry wav'd her hand,
Fair freedom cheer'd the land,
Led on Columbia's band,
    To glorious rest!

Now then, ye sons of song,
Pour the full sound along;
    Who shall control?
For in this western clime,
Freedom shall rise sublime,
'Till ever changing time
    Shall cease to roll.

THE HUE AND CRY.

O YES, my good people, draw near,
    My story surpasses belief,
Yet deign for a moment to hear,
    And assist me to catch a stray thief.

Have you chanc'd a fair damsel to meet,
    Adorn'd like an angel of light,
In a robe that flow'd down to her feet,
    No snow on the mountain so white.

Silver flowers bespangled her shoe,
    Amber locks on her shoulders were spread,
Her waist had a girdle of blue,
    And a beaver plum'd hat had her head.

Her steps an impression scarce leave,
    She bounds o'er the meadow so soon;
Her smile is like Autumn's clear eve,
    And her look as serene as his moon.

She seems to have nothing to blame,
    Deceitless and meek as the dove;
But there lives not a thief of such fame,
    She has pilfer'd below and above.

Her cheek has the blushes of day,
  Her neck has undone the swain's wing,
Her breath has the odors of May,
  And her eye has the dews of the spring.

She has robb'd of its crimson the rose,
  She has dar'd the carnation to strip,
The bee who has plunder'd them knows,
  And would fain fill his hive at her lip.

She has stol'n for her forehead so even,
  All beauty by sea and by land.
She has all the fine azure of Heaven,
  In the veins of her temple and hand.

Yes, yes, she has ransack'd above,
  And beggar'd both nature and art,
She has got all we honor and love,
  And from me she has pilfer'd my heart.

Bring her home, honest friends, bring her home,
  And set her down safe at my door,
Let her once my companion become,
  And I swear she shall wander no more.

Bring her home, and I'll give a reward,
  Whose value can never be told,
More precious than all you regard,
  More in worth than a house full of gold.

A reward such as none but a dunce,
  Such as none but a madman would miss,
O yes, I will give you for once,
  From the charmer you bring me, a kiss.

A LIBERTY SONG.
From a London Paper.

NO longer let kings and base princes decree,
  That men have no rights, nor shall ever be
free:

But let us unite, and our freedom maintain,
Assisted by reason, and honest Tom Paine.

From despots the people no blessings can feel
For their laws are injustice, their arguments steel;
But such laws and such arguments never can gain
The voice of a nation, instructed by Paine.

When kings, who are tyrants, are destin'd to fall,
And the people of England shall lift to the call
Of Liberty's sons—they then will disdain
All the venal revilers of honest Tom Paine.

Then true to his merits let each man be found,
And let virtue, like his, be with victory crown'd;
So may we his ardor and judgment retain,
When to Heaven is call'd the philanthropic Paine.

SONG,

Sung at the Celebration of the Anniversary of the Liberty of the French, at Liverpool, in England.

UNFOLD, Father Time, thy long records unfold,
Of noble atchievments accomplish'd of old;
When men, by the standard of Liberty led,
Undauntedly conquer'd, or cheerfully bled;
But know, 'midst the triumphs these moments reveal,
Their glories shall fade, and their lustre turn pale;
Whilst France rises up, and confirms the decree.
That bids millions rejoice, and a nation be free.

As spring to the field, or as dew to the flower,
To the earth parch'd with heat, as the soft dropping shower;
As health to the wretch who lies languid and wan,
Or as rest to the weary—is Freedom to man.

Where Freedom the light of her countenance gives,
There only he revels, there only he lives.
Seize then the glad moment, and hail the decree,
That bids millions rejoice, and a nation be free.

Too long had oppression and terror entwin'd
Those fancy form'd chains that enslave the free
    mind;
Whilst dark superstition, with nature at strife,
Had lock'd up for ages the fountains of life:
But the demons are fled—the delusion is past—
And reason and virtue have conquer'd at last:
Seize then the glad moment, and hail the decree,
That bids millions rejoice, and a nation be free.

France! we share in the rapture thy bosom that
    fills
Whilst the spirit of Liberty bounds o'er thy hills.
Redundant henceforth, may the purple juice flow,
Prouder wave thy green woods, and thine olive
    trees grow:
For thy brows, may the hand of philosophy twine
(Blest emblems!) the myrtle, the olive, and vine;
And Heaven thro' all ages confirm the decree,
That tears off thy chains, and bids millions be free.

A NEW SONG.

COLUMBIA.

Tune—From the East Breaks the Morn.

WHEN our Fathers came o'e,
    To this wilderness shore,
  They all hazards and dangers despised;
For by tyrants oppress'd,
They came hither in quest,
  Of Freedom, by the brave ever priz'd.

'Twas with labor and toil,
They improved the soil,
   For the wilderness bloom'd like the rose;
And with plenty being crown'd,
To the nations around,
   Terms of friendship and peace did propose.

But, lo! each savage tribe,
With perfidy ally'd!
   Were strangers to peace, friendship, and truth;
For 'tis *Scalps* that they prize,
They are deaf to the cries,
   Of the infant, the aged, or youth.

At length they were quell'd,
And by valor compell'd,
   With submission to sue for a peace;
Thus our fathers renown'd,
Were with victory crown'd,
   And their offspring began to encrease.

So with Liberty bless'd,
They departed to rest,
   And the fruits of their toil left their sons;
Whose firm hearts, like their sires,
Love of Freedom inspires,
   And the shackles of Slavery shun.

For, behold British pride,
With oppression ally'd,
   Soon disturb'd this our envied state:
First, with *Stamps* they oppress'd,
Which, though quickly redress'd,
   They still cherish foul envy and hate.

But the tale is too long,
It would burthen my song,
   To relate how they threaten'd us all;
That unless we'd submit,
To the *terms* they thought fit,
   Without mercy they on us would fall.

That such threats were in vain,
Is well known to each swain,
   Who rambles thro' the lawn or the grove;
For, proud Britons, dismay'd,
Quickly beat the shamade,
   And surrender'd to HIM, whom all love.

No more let Britain boast,
Of her powerful host,
   Nor her sov'reignty over the main;
For we've taught them to know,
That, though num'rous our foe,
   We can *Conquer* again and again.

Now to HIM that rules all,
Who inhabits this ball,
   Our warm gratitude sure will arise;
And, in thanks we'll repeat,
The deliv'rance so great,
   And the *Blessings* of *Liberty* prize.

A NEW SONG.
WASHINGTON.

GOD save great WASHINGTON,
His worth from ev'ry tongue
           Demands applause;
Ye tuneful pow'rs combine,
And each true whig now join,
Whose heart did ne'er resign
           The glorious cause.

Let's sing his martial deeds,
When to Trenton he speeds
           With willing bands;
See there he leads them on,
To glory and renown,
And then with vict'ry's crown
           Triumphant stands.

Next to Princeton he goes,
Where the aſtoniſh'd foes,
           With fear ſtruck pale,
Vainly attempt to ſtand;
For the brave choſen band,
Soon charge them ſword in hand,
           Britons turn tail:

Where e'er the *Hero* comes,
The valiant boaſting ſons
           Of Britain run;
Helter ſkelter they fly,
When *Waſhington* comes nigh,
Or elſe, ſubmiſſively,
           Each grounds his gun.

Let each *Columbian* ſon,
In grateful accents mourn
           The loſs of thoſe,
Who freely bled and fell,
And thus their lives did fell,
For *Liberty* lov'd well,
           And our repoſe.

May *God* the *Congreſs* bleſs
With *power* (nor more nor leſs)
           To make us *great*,
In INDEPENDENCY;
And from all diſcord free,
Grant this may truly be
           Our happy *fate!*

Sweet *Liberty* all hail!
Should *Tyrants* e'er aſſail,
           Grant us thy aid;
May our *poſterity*,
Continue to be *free*,
And may they ever ſee
           The Flag diſplay'd;

ODE,

Sung at the Great Wigwam of the Tammany Society, or Columbian Order, of New-York, on the celebration of the Third Century of the discovery of America by Christopher Columbus, on the 14th October, 1492.

YE Sons of Freedom hail the day,
    That brought a second world to view;
To great Columbus' mem'ry pay
    The praise and honour justly due.
        CHORUS.
    Let the important theme inspire,
    Each breast with patriotic fire.

Long did oppression o'er the world,
    Her sanguine banners wide display:
Dark bigotry her thunders hurl'd,
    And freedom's domes in ruins lay.
        CHORUS.
    Justice and liberty had flown,
    And tyrants call'd the world their own.

Thus heaven our race with pity view'd;
    Resolv'd bright freedom to restore:
And heaven directed o'er the flood,
    Columbus found her on this shore.
        CHORUS.
    O'er the bless'd land with rays divine,
    She shown, and shall forever shine.

Hark! from above, the great decree
    Floats in celestial notes along;
" Columbia ever shall be free—"
    Exulting thousands swell the song.
        CHORUS.
    Patriots revere the great decree,
    Columbia ever shall be free.

Here shall th' enthusiastic love,
  Which freemen to their country owe;
Enkindled, glorious from above,
  In every patriot bosom glow.
        CHORUS.
      Inspire the heart, the arm extend,
      The rights of freedom to defend.

Secure forever, and entire,
  The Rights of Man shall here remain:
No nobles kindle discord's fire,
  Nor despots load with slavery's chain.
        CHORUS.
      Here shall th' oppress'd find sweet repose,
      Since none but tyrants are our foes.

Here commerce shall her sails extend,
  Science diffuse her kindest ray:
Religion's purest flame ascend,
  And peace shall crown each happy day.
        CHORUS.
      Thrice favor'd land, by Heaven design'd,
      A world of blessings for mankind.

Then while we keep this jubilee,
  While seated round this awful shrine,
Columbus' deeds our theme shall be,
  And liberty that gift divine.
        CHORUS.
      Let the transporting theme inspire,
      Each breast with patriotic fire.

ANNA, OR, THE ADIEU.

WHEN the sails catch the breeze, and the an-
        chor is weigh'd,
To bear me from *Anna*, my beautiful maid,
The top-mast ascending, I look for my dear,
And sigh that her features imperfect appear,

Till aided by fancy her charms I still trace,
And for me see the tears trickle down her pale face,
While her handkerchief waving solicits my view,
And I hear her sweet lips sadly sigh out *adieu.*

The pleasing delusion not long can prevail,
Higher rise the proud waves, and more brisk blows the gale;
The gale that regards not the sighs that it bears;
The proud waves still unmov'd, tho' augmented by tears.
Ah! will ye not one single moment delay,
Oh! think from what rapture you bear me away!
Then my eyes strain in vain my dear *Anna* to view,
And a tear drops from each, as I sigh out *adieu.*

Yet some comfort it gives to my agoniz'd mind,
That I still see the land where I left her behind;
The land that gave birth to my charmer and me,
Tho' less'ning, my eyes beem with pleasure to see;
'Tis the casket that holds all that's dear to my heart,
'Tis the haven where yet we shall meet ne'er to part,
If the fates are propitious to lovers so true;
But if not, dearest *Anna!* a long, long *adieu!*

ODE

On the DEATH of Dr. FRANKLIN.

AIR—" *Return enraptured Hours.*"

THE fairest flow'rets bring
   In all their vernal bloom,
And let the sweets of spring
   Adorn great *Franklin's* tomb.
The patriot's toil is done,
   At length his labours cease;
The unfading crown is won,
   His sun descends in peace.

The sons of science grieve,
  Each patriot heaves a sigh,
Yet scarcely can believe
  Such worth could ever die:
No! deathless is that name,
  Whose glory must increase,
And *Franklin's* splendid fame,
  With time alone can cease.

While nimble light'nings fly,
  While awful thunders roll,
While meteors gild the sky,
  And dart from pole to pole,
Mankind will still admire,
  When *Franklin's* name they hear,
Who snatch'd celestial fire,
  And broke th' oppressor's spear.

Thro' ev'ry future age,
  Whilst hist'ry holds her pen,
She'll rank our honour'd sage
  Among the first of men;
And when she counts her sons,
  Who've earn'd immortal fame,
Shall next to *Washington's*,
  Record great *Franklin's* name.

SONG,

Written on the taking of St. JOHN's.

Air—"*Hark! Hark! the Joy Inspiring Horn.*"

HARK! hark! the joyful News is come,
  Sound, sound the trumpet, beat the drum,
    Let manly joy abound,
Where freedom's sacred ensigns wave,
Supported by the free and brave,
    There vict'ry is found.

From east from west, from south from north,
America's brave sons come forth,
    All terrible in arms.
Their right and freedom to maintain;
They dauntless tread the bloody plain,
    And laugh at war's alarms.

Kind Providence, our troops inspire
With more than Greek or Roman fire,
    Our cause, therefore, prevails.
Favour'd by Heav'n, a free-born few,
Tyrannic legions shall subdue,
    For justice seldom fails.

Let joyful temp'rate bowls pass round,
And songs to their just praise resound,
    Who have their valour shewn.
To Putnam, and to Montgomery,
To Wooster, Gates, to Wayne, to Lee,
    And glorious WASHINGTON.

On the BIRTH-DAY of WASHINGTON.

AMERICANS rejoice!
  While songs employ each voice,
    Let trumpets sound:
The thirteen stripes display,
On flags and streamers gay,
'Tis WASHINGTON birth day,
    Joy shall abound.

From scenes of rural peace,
From affluence and ease,
    At Freedom's call;
A hero from his birth,
Great *Washington* stands forth,
The scourge of *George* and *North*,
    And tyrants all.

Those renown'd chiefs of old,
Cæsars and heroes bold,
      Who realms have won,
Smit by his brighter blaze,
Hide their diminish'd rays,
And yield the palm of praise
      To WASHINGTON.

The silver trump of fame,
His glories shall proclaim,
      'Till time is done ;
Genius, with taste refin'd,
Valor, with courage join'd,
'Bove all, an honest mind,
      Has WASHINGTON.

Long may he live to see,
This land of liberty,
      Flourish in peace ;
Long may he live to prove
A grateful people's love,
And late to Heaven remove,
      Where joys ne'er cease.

Fill the glass to the brink,
Washington's health we'll drink,
      'Tis his birth day :
Glorious deeds he has done,
By him our cause is won,
Long live our WASHINGTON,
      Huzza! huzza!

THE INDIAN STUDENT.

A celebrated NEW SONG.

FROM Susquehannah's utmost springs,
   Where savage tribes pursue their game,
His blanket ty'd with yellow strings
   The shephard of the forest came.

Not long before a wandering priest
    Exprest his wish with visage sad,
Ah why he cried, in Satan's waste,
    Ah why detain so fine a lad.

In yankee land there stands a town
    Where learning may be purchas'd low,
Exchange his blanket for a gown,
    And let the lad to college go.

From long debate the council rose,
    And viewing Shallum's tricks with joy,
To Harvard hall o'er drifted snows,
    They sent the tawny colour'd boy.

Awhile he wrote, awhile he read,
    Awhile attended grammar rules,
An Indian savage, so well bred,
    Great credit promis'd to the schools.

Some thought he would in law excel,
    Some said in physic he would shine,
And some who lik'd him passing well,
    Beheld in him a sound divine.

But those of more discerning eye,
    Even then could other prospects show;
They saw him lay his Virgil by,
    To wander with his dearer bow.

The tedious hours of study spent,
    The heavy moulded lecture done,
He to the woods a hunting went,
    But sigh'd to see the setting sun.

The shady banks, the purling streams,
    The woody wild his heart possest,
The dewy lawn his morning dreams,
    In fancy's finest colours drest.

Ah why he cry'd did I forsake
  My native woods for gloomy walls,
The silver stream, the limpid lake,
  For musty books, and college halls.

A little could my wants supply,
  Can wealth or honor give me more?
Or will the Sylvan God deny
  The humble treat he gave before?

Where nature's ancient forests grow,
  And mingled laurel never fades,
My heart is fixt, and I must go
  To die among my native shades.

He spake, and to the western springs,
  His gown discharg'd, his money spent,
His blanket tied with yellow strings,
  The shepherd of the forest went.

Returning to his rural plain,
  The Indians welcom'd him with joy:
The council took him home again,
  And blest the tawny colour'd boy.

LIBERTY TREE.

WHILE war's crimson carnage is drenching the plains
Of Europe, and tyrants are forging their chains,
Our brethren to shackle, our song still should be
Success to the growth of the Liberty Tree!

On the blood of "their people" have tyrants long fed,
While to swell their curst coffers that blood hath been shed;
But their teeth, lo! they gnash, while in anguish they see
Nations hailing triumphant the Liberty Tree!

Yes! the time is approaching, and fast rolls along,
When "air, earth and ocean," shall ring with the
   song,
And *The Great Common Father* his children shall see,
Auspiciously blest under Liberty Tree!

For tho' clouds for a while dim the glory of France,
Still her heroes invincible brandish the lance
Of war, and her foes, in confusion, shall see
O'er creation expanding the Liberty Tree!

With your gen'rous Franks, our hearts they do beat,
Sympathize in distress, and vict'ry greet,
Still wishing the joyful glad æra to see,
When the shade's universal of Liberty Tree!

Then go on with the glorious work you've begun,
Independency take for your SHIELD and SUN;
That despots may tremble with dread while they
   see
The branches extending of Liberty Tree!

Lo! their slaves now they muster, and think to
   prevail,
But Freedom's victorious, tho' millions assail,
Which hastens the moon, when, in jubilee,
Mankind shall rejoice under Liberty Tree!

May Truth, Light and Virtue, descend from above,
And fix the fair empire of Reason and Love!
From king-croft, and priest-craft, mankind they
   free,
And forever entwine round the Liberty Tree!

The plant of Columbia's soil the produce,
Of its fruit how ennobling, and mild is the juice,
Which, the moment they taste it, gives mortals to
   see
What Beauties are center'd in Liberty Tree!

No rays of false splendor, reflected from courts,
Can light a desire in Columbian hearts,
Such gewgaws of pride, and ambition to see,
By Reason united to Liberty Tree.

Columbia, while bless'd with the fair smiles of peace,
Stands a rival in glory with Rome and with Greece;
Let her sons then forget not "they fought to be free,"
And in blood that they planted their Liberty Tree!

Having faith that e'er long the whole world will enjoy
What the shade of ages shall never destroy;
Turks, Africans, Russians, enlighten'd, shall see,
And pluck the fair blossoms of Liberty Tree!

That soon the mild goddess, sweet Peace with her wings
Shall shelter the globe, and e'en tyrants and kings,
To citizens chain'd, with rapture shall see,
The wide spreading glory of Liberty Tree!

That east, west, north and south, shall catch the glad sound,
And loud Hymns of Freedom re-echo around:
While the one universal grand chorus shall be,
May immortality flourish our Liberty Tree!

Albany (N. York) June 26, 1793.

SONG.

WHY stands the tear in Mara's eye,
    And why that touching, pensive air;
For whom, dear Mara, dost thou sigh,
    For whom let fall that virgin tear?

Say hath some youth to virtue lost,
   Beguil'd thee of thy tender heart,
Then of thy favors made his boast,
   And pierc'd thee with detraction's dart?

If so, dear Mara, check the sigh,
   That rises from thy wounded heart;
No longer let thy dewy eye,
   The tale of inward grief impart.

The youth who slights thy virgin love,
   And throws detraction's venom'd dart;
Believe me, Mara, soon will prove,
   What anguish rends a guilty heart!

THE CAMP OF BEAUTY.
A NEW SONG.

COME all, ye lovely virgins, come,
  Obedient to the beat of drum,
     Which calls for volunteers:
Hark! hark! the joy inspiring sound
Will make each captur'd heart rebound,
     And chace all qualmish fears.
Then haste to Beauty's Camp away,
Where Cupid arm'd in proud array,
     With quivers, bows and darts,
Invites you all—come follow me,
To happiness and victory,
     To conquer soldiers hearts.
Come all, ye lovely virgins, &c.

Each blooming maid, who wants a mate,
To bless her in the bridal state,
     Not bent on leading apes,
To Beauty's Camp with me repair,
For O, how happy is the fair,
     Who such a doom escapes!

Reflect then—O reflect on this,
And fly to meet the proffer'd bliss,
      That Hymen holds in view;
For, chear'd by Love's delighting ray,
Each virgin fair may glad obey
      My charming rat-tat-too!
Come all, ye lovely, &c.

See Venus, Cupid, Hymen too,
(Who form a league in aid of you)
      Encamp'd in Beauty's field:
Soon to your bright enchanting eyes,
Supported by such great allies,
      The bravest heart must yield.
For till in parley they produce,
In Beauty's Camp a flag of truce,
      The cannon of your charms
Shall ply their breast at such a rate,
They'll soon surrender to their fate,
      And gladly club their arms.
Then come, ye lovely virgins, &c.

THE TENDER's HOLD.

WHILE landmen wander uncontroul'd,
    And boast the rights of freemen,
O! view the Tender's loathsome hold,
    Where droop your injur'd seamen;
Dragg'd by oppression's savage grasp,
    From every dear connection,
Midst putrid air, O! hear them gasp,
    And mark their deep dejection.

      CHORUS.
Blush then, ye mean, ye pension'd host,
    Who wallow in profusion,
For yon foul cell proves all your boast
    To be but mere delusion.

If freedom be our birth-right, say,
  Why are not all protected?
Why is the hand of ruffian sway
  'Gainst seamen thus directed?
Is this your proof of British rights?
  Is this rewarding bravery?
O shame! to boast your tars exploits,
  Yet doom those tars to slavery.
                    Blush then, &c.

O! that ambition's callous train,
  Who wish to shine in story,
Who tinge with blood the earth and main,
  And call their havoc glory,
O! that these scourgers of the world,
  Who smile at man's undoing,
Might from their lordly seats be hurl'd,
  And taste the cup of ruin.
                    Blush then, &c.

Are Britons free?—ye vaunting crew,
  Who damn all reformation,
Deep in the Tender's Hold, O! view,
  The guardians of your nation:
Yes, view them thus in durance laid,
  Though void of all transgression,
Then say, could Russia's bloody jade
  Display more foul oppression?
                    Blush then, &c.

But just return'd from noxious skies,
  And winter's raging ocean,
To land the sun-burnt seaman flies,
  Impell'd by strong emotion;
His much loved Kate, his children dear,
  Around him cling delighted,
When lo! the impressing fiends appear,
  And every joy is blighted.
                    Blush then, &c.

Thus from each soft endearment torn,
   Here view the seaman languish,
His wife, his children left forlorn,
   The prey of bitter anguish;
'Reft of those arms whose vigorous strength
   Their shed from want defended,
They droop, and all their woes at length
   Are in a workhouse ended.
              Blush then, &c.

Mark then, ye minions of a court,
   Who prate of freedom's blessing,
Yet every hell-born war support,
   And vindicate impressing;
A time will come, when things like you,
   Mere baubles of creation,
No more shall make mankind pursue,
   The work of devastation.

CHORUS.

Blush then, ye mean, ye pensioned host,
   Who wallow in profusion,
For yon foul cell proves all your boast
   To be but mere delusion.

An ODE,

For the FOURTH of JULY.

(Composed by Mr. Lathrop, of Boston.)

FILL! fill to WASHINGTON,
   Liberty's valiant son,
      Let the toast pass!
From each convivial band;
From this vast, grateful land,
His deeds due praise demand,
      Fill, fill the glass!

Heaven on our labour smiles,
Fair Freedom crowns our toils,
  And justice reigns;
Peace shines with cheerful mein,
Happiness beams serene,
And plenty, cloath'd in green,
  Blesses our plains.

On ocean's swelling tide,
See our ships proudly ride,
  Laden with wealth!
Round fair Columbia's seat,
Virtues and graces meet,
Pleasures which make life sweet,
  Honour and health.

O'er Europe's fields afar,
Bold thousands rush to war,
  With dauntless souls!
In Freedom's glorious cause,
To save their rights and laws,
From grim oppression's jaws,
  War's thunder rolls.

Such was the god-like fire,
Which did our breasts inspire,
  When great in arms—
Heroes like Jove in might,
Rag'd in the bloody fight,
Throughout the realms of night,
  Spread dire alarms.

Down fell old slav'ry power,
Thank God! to rise no more,
  To curse the world.
In the abyss of hell,
Where kindred furies dwell,
And in mad ravings yell,
  Groaning, she's hurl'd!

Now war's rude clangours cease,
And olive-scept'red peace
    Reigns all around;
Raise high the cheerful song,
Heaven shall the notes prolong,
And the angelick throng
    Echo the sound!

A NEW SONG,

On the FOURTH of JULY.

INDEPENDENCE! how bright are the blessings
    you give!
They teach hapless mortals in comfort to live;
Remote from ambition and folly's career,
No *monarch* we flatter, no *nation* we fear.

The gun, drum, and trumpet have yielded to peace,
And our soil every year boasts plenteous increase;
Gay commerce securely now hoists the bold sail,
And, by Liberty blest, can Americans fail?

Her efforts now industry fully displays;
And on our exertions proud foreigners gaze.
Then let all degrees reap th' expected reward,
Independence we gain'd—*Independence* we'll guard.

On the *Fourth of July* the blest guardian appear'd,
Which patriot bosoms with confidence cheer'd.
Your glasses then fill, ye who liberty favour,
And this be your toast—" *Independence forever.*"

Now *Monarchy* droops—*Aristocracy* too;
And all with content may their labours pursue:
Over us the bright star of blest Freedom arose,
Which enlightens our friends, and shall bless e'en
    our foes.

ODE,

On Gen. WASHINGTON's *Birth-day.*

HAIL to the Sun, whose circling ray
  Once more revolves the happy day,
That gave our HERO birth:
Prepare the feast, in pairs advance,
To raise the song, or lead the dance
  To jolity and mirth.

CHORUS.

Blow the trumpet, sound the flute,
Tune the viol, strike the lute,
And let every free-born soul
Chant his name from pole to pole.

Ambition fir'd the chiefs of old
To fight for empire or for gold,
  How few for Liberty:
But he was born by Heav'n design'd
To scourge the oppressors of mankind,
  And set th' oppressed free.

Cæsar and Philip's frantic son
With arms and chains the world over run,
  To gratify their pride;
Benevolence and valor join'd,
Display the greatness of his mind,
  And all his actions guide.

Nassau forsook his native land,
Great Britain's ruin to withstand,
  And he the nation sav'd:
Great Malbro' led her conquering force
Where nothing could retard his course,
  And ev'ry danger brav'd.

William's high deeds a crown obtain'd;
A prince's title Malbro' gain'd:
  But greater is *his* claim—

Thirteen United People's prayers,
Their soldiers hearts, their senate's cares,
  Are offer'd all for *him*.

Propitious victory has spread
A grove of laurels round his head,
  And peace his conquest crown'd :
May no malignant spirit dare,
With baneful breath, God grant my prayer,
  His fame or peace to wound.

But may good angels near him wait,
To bear him late, O very late,
  From hence to realms above ;
And may he be permitted there,
As with his arm he freed us here,
  To speed us with his love.

Chorus—Blow the trumpet, &c.

RECITATIVE.

Had I my favorite prior's happy vein,
I'd sing his triumphs in a noble strain ;
Nassau or Malbro' should not brighter shine
In bolder figure, or a smoother line ;
Ensigns and trophies shou'd adorn his bowers,
And Vernon's Mount rise high as Blenheim's towers.

Chorus—Blow the trumpet, &c.

To COLUMBIA's FAVORITE SON.

GREAT Washington ! the Hero's come,
  Each heart exulting, hears the sound ;
Thousands to their Deliverer throng,
And shout him welcome all around.
  Now in full chorus join the song,
  And shout aloud great Washington.

Q

There view Columbia's favorite son,
Her Father, Saviour, Friend, and Guide,
There see th' immortal Washington,
His country's glory, boast, and pride.
    Now in full chorus, &c.

When th' impending storm of war,
Thick clouds and darkness hid our way—
Great Washington, our polar star,
Arose—and all was light as day.
    Now in full chorus, &c.

'Twas on yon plains thy value rose,
And ran like fire, from man to man.
'Twas here thou humbled Paria's foes,
And chac'd whole legions to the main.
    Now in full chorus, &c.

Thro' countless dangers, toils, and cares,
Our Hero led us safely on—
With matchless skill directs the wars,
'Till victory cries—the day's his own.
    Now in full chorus, &c.

His country sav'd—the contest o'er,
Sweet peace restor'd, his toils to crown,
The warrior to his native shore
Returns, and tills his fertile ground.
    Now in full chorus, &c.

But soon Columbia call'd him forth,
Again to save her sinking fame,
To take the helm, and by his worth,
To make her an immortal name.
    Now in full chorus, &c.

Nor yet alone through Paria's shores,
Her fame—her mighty trumpet's blown,
E'en Europe, Afric, Asia hears
And emulate the deeds he's done.
    Now in full chorus, &c.

ANTHEM,

For the FOURTH of JULY.

I.

HAIL! the first, the greatest blessing,
　God hath given to man below;
Hail to freedom, independence,
Boundless, boundless may they flow!
Favor'd people, blest Columbia, happy nation,
Freedom, peace, be ever thine.

II.

Give to God the pow'r and glory,
　Own 'twas his almighty hand,
Which from Britain's isle conducted,
　Patriot heroes to this land;
Then a desert, waste and howling, then a desert,
　Now the asylum of the Earth.

III.

Who subdu'd the warlike savage,
　Nimrod hunter of the wood?
Who, amid the storm of battle,
　In the cloud or pillar stood?
'Twas Jehovah, 'twas Jehovah, 'twas Jehovah,
　Universal nature's Lord.

IV.

When a parent to the children
Scorpions gave instead of bread,
Who, educing good from evil,
Hungry babes with plenty fed?
Shout Jehovah, sing Jehovah, shout Jehovah,
Praises, praises be to him.

V.

High exalted, firmly seated,
　Independent, sovereign, free,
May Columbia's grateful millions
　Glory, Glory give to thee.
Might, dominion, praises, blessing, glory, glory,
All the glory, Lord, be thine.

VI.

Ev'ry nation, all the kingdoms,
Bless, oh bless, eternal fire!
Man adoring; angels hymning,
Rapture feeling, transports shouting, praises sounding,
Hail! they cry, amen! amen!

The RAISING:

A new Song *for* Federal Mechanics.

I.

COME muster, my lads, your mechanical tools,
   Your saws and your axes, your hammers and rules;
Bring your mallets and planes, your level and line,
And plenty of pins of American pine;
   For our roof we will raise, and our song still shall be,
   A Government firm, and our Citizens free.

II.

Come, up with *the plates*, lay them firm on the wall,
Like the people at large, they're the ground-work of all;
Examine them well, and see that they're sound,
Let no rotten parts in our building be found;
   For our roof we will raise, and our song still shall be,
   Our Government firm, and our Citizens free.

III.

Now hand up *the girders*, lay each in his place,
Between them *the joists* must divide all the space;
Like assembly-men, *these* should lye level along,
Like *girders*, our senate prove loyal and strong;
   For our roof we will raise, and our song still shall be,
   A Government firm, over Citizens free.

IV.

The rafters now frame—your *king-posts* and *braces*,
And drive your pins home, to keep all in their places;

Let wisdom and strength in the fabric combine,
And your pins be all made of American pine;
*For our roof we will raise, and our song still shall be,
A Government firm, over Citizens free.*

V.

Our *king-posts* are judges—how upright they stand,
Supporting the *braces*, the laws of the land;
The laws of the land, which divide right from wrong,
And strengthen the weak, by weak'ning the strong;
*For our roof we will raise, and our song still shall be,
Laws equal and just, for a People that's free.*

VI.

Lo! Up with the rafters—each frame is a state!
How nobly they rise! their span, too, how great!
From the north to the south, o'er the whole they extend,
And rest on the walls, while the walls they defend!
*For our roof we will raise, and our song still shall be,
Combined in strength, yet as Citizens free.*

VII.

Now enter the *purlins*, and drive your pins through,
And see that your joints are drawn home, and all true;
The *purlins* will bind all the rafters together,
The strength of the whole shall defy wind and weather;
*For our roof we will raise, and our song still shall be,
United as States, but as Citizens free.*

VIII.

Come, raise up the turret, our glory and pride;
In the centre it stands, o'er the whole to preside;
The Sons of Columbia shall view with delight
Its pillars and arches, and towering height;
*Our roof is now rais'd, and our song still shall be,
A federal Head, o'er a People still free.*

IX.

Huzza! my brave boys, our work is complete,
The world shall admire Columbia's fair seat;

Its strength against tempest and time shall be proof,
And thousands shall come to dwell under our *Roof*.
  Whilst we drain the deep bowl, our toast still shall be,
  Our Government firm, and our Citizens free.

A SONG.

HAIL, Freedom all hail! on the top of Mount Bleed,
Where Grand Master *Warren* was destin'd to bleed,
We saw thee in spirit with favor of Heav'n,
The Hero and Patriot to whom it was giv'n,
Mid clouds and thick darkness to lead forth the day,
Which Europe new lightens with liberty's ray.

Hail, Freedom, all hail! thy life kindling beams,
Which broke on Monnt Breed, sheds of reason the gleams,
Ov'r kingdoms and nations loug hid from its light,
Lo, darkness recedeth, and past is the night:
To nature's wide limits thy splendour shall blaze,
And myriads on millions salute thee with praise.

Hail, Freedom, all hail! rise on pinions out spread:
From France be thy course thro' the Universe sped;
Teach monarchs and priests, with the nobles of earth,
To own that from Heav'n springs Liberty's birth:
Whilst the south and north, the east and the west,
With Liberty, Life, Peace, and Freedom are blest.

PATRIOTISM,

An ODE, *in honor of those who distinguished themselves in the late* WAR.

YE patriots, listen to my strain,
Nor thou, philosophy, disdain

A theme, which every mind muſt raiſe;
Which angels might deſcend to praiſe.
Methinks I hear the ſong again,
Glory to God, and Peace to Men.

What merit ſhall I firſt record,
The patriots' eloquence or ſword?
Great Waſhington, in valor's field,
Compell'd our haughty foes to yield.
Franklin, in France, who mildly ſhone,
Prov'd both Minervas are our own.

Of thoſe who oft their courage tried,
Who nobly liv'd, or nobly died.
Good Waſhington we own ſupreme,
The ſoldier's pride, the patriot's theme.
He knew in battle to excel;
The arts of peace he knows as well.

How many deathleſs praiſe have won!
Bold Adams—gentler Dickinſon—
Hancock's determin'd ſoul, combin'd
With Jefferſon's enlighten'd mind.
Our breaſts with worth were taught to glow,
And honor'd foreign Rochambeau.

O France! thy virtues we confeſs;
May Heaven reward thee with ſucceſs!
Thy ſtruggles let the world revere;
Fayette is thine—and canſt thou fear!
France taught our haughty foes to bow;
In freedom we inſtruct her now.

Still let us ev'ry tribute give
To thoſe who died, or thoſe who live;
To thoſe who felt the battle's rage,
Or now in peaceful arts engage.
To Gates immortal praiſe be given,
Whilſt Warren's ſpirits reſt in Heaven;

Ye soldiers who in battle glow'd!
Ye artists, who true genius shew'd!
Ye statesmen, firm at once and just,
Whether ye live or rest in dust,
The muse shall crown you with applause:
Great were your deeds, and just your cause.

  I sing (attend me, age and youth!)
The strains of glory and of truth.
See! a *new government* appears,
Doubts to dispel, and banish fears:
And see! (whilst rapture warms each breast)
The *star of empire in the West!*

On the FOURTH of JULY.

ON the basis of fame Columbia stands,
   Her pendants refulgent in foreign lands;
Ages remote her exploits will extol,
And waft the glad tidings from pole to pole.
The records of Greece, and the annals of Rome,
Are hush'd in silence, and mute as the tomb.
Since nature's grand fiat spoke realms to be,
And chaos gave way to land and to sea;
A more lucid æra time ne'er enroll'd,
Nor nations such laurels did e'er behold.
From the verge of space to the centre of spheres,
Columbia's thunders shall wake distant fears;
And th' oak, which now nods in forests unknown,
Shall visit all climes, and count them its own.
Where *Sol* baths his steeds in the western main,
And from Indus's waves emerges again;
The *Stripes* triumphant shall ride o'er the sea,
And the trumpet of fame echo us—*free.*
May those who preside o'er councils and states,
With olives expanded, end our debates;
And Ceres her gifts profusely bestow,
'Till the exit of time, and all things below.

ODE,
On the FOURTH of JULY.

COME all ye sons of song,
  Pour the full sound along,
     In joyful strains.
Beneath these western skies,
See a new empire rise,
Bursting, with glad surprise,
     Tyrannick chains.

Liberty, with keen eye,
Pierc'd the blue vaulted sky,
     Resolv'd us free ;
From her imperial seat,
Beheld the bleeding state,
Approv'd THIS DAY's debate,
     And firm decree.

Sublime, in awful form,
Amid the whirling storm,
     The Goddess stood :
She saw with pitying eye,
War's tempest raging high,
Our heroes bravely die,
     In fields of blood.

High on his shining car,
Mars, the stern god of war,
     Our struggle blest.
Soon victory wav'd her hand,
Fair Fredom cheer'd the land,
Led on Columbia's band,
     To glorious rest.

Now then, ye sons of song,
Pour the full sound along ;
     Who shall controul ?
For in this western clime,
Freedom shall rise sublime,
'Till ever changing time
     Shall cease to roll !

SONG.

A new Method of driving our Enemies without the expence of powder, shot, &c. as lately practised at Brighton (England.)

Tune—"*Derry Down.*"

LET the foes of Great-Britain now wantonly brag,
Let them show their grim teeth, and their tails let them wag;
For if Brighton's militia once have them in view,
They'll be sent away briskly, with boo, d—me boo,
   Sing boo, boo, d—me, boo.

'Twas by that a wise Doctor was turn'd from the play,
For preaching his duty, on a Sabbath day;
Quick at him these *glorious veterans* flew,
And made him retreat with a boo, d—me boo.
   Sing boo, &c.

So after the Doctor was turn'd from the house,
They proceeded to offer the same to his spouse;
She was push'd by the shoulder by one of the crew,
With a "right about face, Madam," boo, d—me, boo.
   Sing boo, &c.

Come then, let us rejoice, since a way we have got
To destroy all our foes without powder or shot:
We have no need in blood our brave hands to imbrue,
For we'll send them all off with a boo, d—me. boo.
   Sing boo, &c.

Let us heartily thank then, these sons of defence,
For showing at once both their courage and sense:
Pray what more could contribute their wisdom to shew,
Than this learned expression of boo, d—me, boo.
   Sing boo, &c.

If the French ever dare on our coasts to appear,
We'll send them away with a flea in their ear;
To our fears and our foes then we'll all bid adieu,
As we're so well defended by boo, d—me, boo.
      Sing boo, &c.

THE DISH OF TEA.

LET some in grog place their delight,
 O'er bottled porter waste the night,
  Or sip the rosy wine;
   A dish of tea—more pleases me,
   Yields softer joys—provokes less noise,
  And breeds no base design.

From China's clime this present brought,
Enlivens every power of thought,
  Rigs many a ship for sea;
   Old maids it warms—young widows charms,
   And misses' men—not one in ten,
  But court them for their tea.

When throbbing pains assail my head,
And dulness o'er my brain is spread,
  The muse no longer kind;
   A single sip—dispels the hyp,
   To chase the gloom—fresh spirits come,
  The flood-tide of the mind.

When worn with toil, or vext with care,
Let Susan but this draught prepare,
  And I forget my pain;
   This magic bowl—revives the soul,
   With gentle sway—bids care be gay,
  Nor mounts to croud the brain.

If learned men the truth would speak,
They prize it far beyond their Greek,

More fond attention pay ;
  No Hebrew root—so well can suit,
  More quickly taught—less dearly bought,
And studied twice a day.

This leaf from distant regions sprung,
Puts life into the female tongue,
  And aids the cause of love.
    Such power has *tea*—o'er bond and free,
    Which priests admire—delights the 'squire,
  And Galen's sons approve.

―――

"MARCHE DES MARSEILLOIS."

Attempted in English.

ARISE ye generous youths of France,
  And mark the glory of this day ;
'Gainst us the tyrant throng advance,
  And high the bloody flag display. *(twice.)*
Our field ferocious hirelings dare,
  And send fierce howlings to the sky ;
They come ! and from your arms they tear
  Your pratling babes, who bleeding die !

    To arms, ye patriot band,
      In firm battalions rise ;
        March on, march on,
      Lest blood disguise
    Your own native land.
      We march, we march,
        Lest blood disguise
    Our own native land.

What would this herd of conjur'd kings,
  Vile slaves and traitors, ghastly throng !
For whom the chain ignoble brings
  The bondage we have suffered long. *(twice.)*

In vengeance, French, let every breast
  With swelling transport ceaseless burn,
Fair freedom teaches to detest
  The slavery they bid return.
                    To arms, &c.

What! would these proud outlandish foes
  Be legislators in our land?
What! would these hireling crowds oppose
  And lay in dust our warlike band! *(twice.)*
Great God! shall then the enslaving rod·
  Subject us to our former state?
Shall a vile despot's sov'reign nod
  Decide at will our abject fate!
                    To arms, &c.

Our warriors now the glory share,
  By them you fall, by them succeed;
Spare then the wretched victims, spare,
  We arm to die or make you bleed. *(twice.)*
But lo! these sanguinary lords
  Joyous exert their savage pow'r,
These bloody tygers lift their swords,
  And their own country's peace devour.
                    To arms, &c.

Tremble, proud tyrants, traitors blush,
  Quick, quick resign the victor's plume,
The arm of justice, rais'd to crush,
  Descends, and you must meet your doom. *(twice.)*
All, all are soldiers now in France,
  And should we fall, new legions rise,
Our youth to join the fight advance,
  And learn all danger to despise.
                    To arms, &c.

       ·[THE CHILDREN.]
With joy we will assume the trust,
  When down death's hill our fathers roll,
             R

Then shall we find their sacred dust
   Will animate th' aspiring soul. *(twice.)*
Less zealous to survive our sires,
   Than share the death we all contemn,
Their sons a glorious pride inspires
   T'avenge their wrongs, or follow them.
                              To arms, &c.

Oh! "sacred love of country," aid
   Our vengeful arms, our footsteps guide;
And Liberty, celestial maid,
   Adhere to thy defenders' side. *(twice.)*
When victory our tents shall leave,
   To spread the joyous tidings round,
Thy triumph and our fame shall give
   Our enemies their dying wound.
                              To arms, &c.

Our native soil and social love
   Together limit our desires;
Then ever let our souls improve
   The glow the virtuous wish inspires. *(twice.)*
By union shall our pow'r increase,
   Our enemies shall hug their chains,
And then the happy French shall cease
   To chant the harsh incongruous strain.
                              To arms, &c.

A SONG.

On the FOURTH of JULY.

[Tune—Great Washington.]

HAIL thou auspicious day,
   Long may America
      Thy praise resound:

This is a nation's birth,
Freemen come raise your mirth,
See tyrants quit the earth,
    When Freedom's found.

Now eighteen years are spent
Since (O the great event)
    America was freed;
We despots did withstand,
And drove the slavish band,
And in Columbia's land
    Made tyrants bleed.

Behold brave Gallia's sons,
They fear not dukes nor dons,
    Princes nor slaves;
They Freedom will maintain,
'Till they their rights obtain,
Great vict'ry shall they gain,
    In spite of knaves.

May Heaven their cause still bless,
And grant their arms success,
    Down be kings hurl'd;
May all their rulers prove,
Men who fair Freedom love,
May despots all be drove
    Out of the world.

Prussians will fight no more,
Austrians will soon give o'er,
    And quit the field;
Dutchmen are weary grown,
Spaniards their weakness own,
Britons may fight alone,
    But soon shall yield.

See Britain's glory fade,
Ever by knaves betray'd,
    While kings remain;

But soon the cry shall spread,
" Down with the monarchs' head,
" Mankind must no more dread
      Priestcraft nor chains."

Frenchmen your courage raise,
You shall have lasting praise
      All the world round:
Millions unborn shall bless
Your acts of faithfulness,
Dispelling wretchedness
      Where men are bound.

Dem'crats, we bid you hail!
Ne'er let the spirit fail
      Of seventy-six.
If tories should intrude,
Banish their envious brood,
This will prove lasting good,
      Peace firm to fix.

Americans all rejoice,
Raise up your cheerful voice,
      Let cannon roar;
Tell princes, lords, and kings,
Freedom each blessing brings,
Hark how her glory rings,
      All the world o'er.

AN ODE,
For the FOURTH of JULY.
(To the Tune of Columbia.)

AMERICA's birth-day bids Freemen arise,
    And sound in loud triumph her fame to the
      skies;
Independence! thy standard to Liberty's shore
Shall ever be welcome 'till time is no more.

May festive oblations forever adorn
The *Fourth of July*, the bright star of our morn;
And may each Annivers'ry illumine the mind,
And knowledge diffuse thro' the mass of mankind.

May the Ruler of nations bid discord to cease
In our Congress and Senate, and bless us with
   Peace;
And may infinite wisdom inspire them to plan
Such laws as insure the *Divine Rights of Man!*

May the despots of Europe, with armies combin'd
Against sacred Freedom, defeats ever find;
May discord in council their diets confound,
And their subjects awake at fair Liberty's sound.

May wisdom direct the Convention of France,
Pure Liberty's cause and 'Man's Rights' to ad-
  vance;
May her armies, still firm and united as one,
Complet in full conquest the task they've begun.

May virtue secure us from evils to come,
From tyrants abroad, and from despots at home;
May the foes of Columbia be crush'd in the dust,
'Till haughty *Great-Britain shall learn to be just!*

AN ODE,
For the FOURTH of JULY.

'TIS done! the edict past by Heav'n decreed,
 And Hancock's name confirms the glorious
  deed.
   On this auspicious morn
   Was *Independence* born,
    Propitious day!
Hail the United States of blest America.

CHORUS.

Fly, swift wing'd fame,
The news proclaim;
From shore to shore,
Let cannons roar,
And joyful voices shout Columbia's name.

See haughty Britain, sending hosts of foes,
With vengeance arm'd, our Freedom to oppose;
But *Washington the Great*,
Dispell'd impending fate,
And spurn'd each plan;
Americans, combine to hail the god-like man!
Fly, swift wing'd fame, &c.

Let Saratoga's crimson plains declare
The deeds of Gates, that "thunder-bolt of war;"
His trophies grac'd the field,
He made whole armies yield—
A vet'ran band;
In vain did Burgoyne strive his valor to withstand.
Fly, swift wing'd fame, &c.

Now York-Town's heights attract our wond'ring eyes,
Where loud artill'ry rends the lofty skies:
There Washington commands,
With Gallia's chosen bands,
A war-like train;
Like Homer's conquering gods, they thunder o'er the plain.
Fly, swift wing'd fame, &c.

Pale terror marches on, with solemn stride,
Cornwallis trembles, Britain's boasted pride;
He, and his armed hosts,
Surrender all their posts
To Washington,
The friend of Liberty—Columbia's favorite son.
Fly, swift wing'd fame, &c.

Now from Mount Vernon's peaceful shades again
The Hero comes, with thousands in his train;
   'Tis Washington the Great
    Must fill the chair of state,
     Columbia cries;
Each tongue the glorious name re-echoes to the
   skies. Fly, swift wing'd fame, &c.

Now shall the useful arts of peace prevail,
And commerce flourish, favor'd by each gale;
    Discord forever cease!
    Let Liberty and Peace
     And Justice reign;
For Washington protects the scientific train.
     Fly, swift wing'd fame, &c.

COLUMBIA RELIEVED.

Tune—The Death of General Wolfe.

TO a mouldering cavern, the mansion of woe,
 Columbia did often repair;
She tore the fresh laurel that bloom'd on her brow,
 And threw it aside in despair.
She wept for the fate of her sons that were slain,
 When the flames of fierce battle were spread,
When discord and carnage, relaxing the reign,
 Rode smiling o'er mountains of dead.

II.

As thus the bright Goddess revolv'd in her breast
 The wrongs which her country had borne,
A form more than human the Genius addrest,
 " Ah cease, fair Columbia, to mourn.
Now lift up thine eyes, and thy records behold,
 Inscrib'd in the archives of fame,

The *Fourth of July*, in
  Foretells the renow~~

III.

From the caverns of darkness thy day-spring shall
    dawn,
  Ye kings and ye tyrants, beware;
Your names shall decay like the vapours of morn,
  Or vanish in phantoms of air:
They temple, O Freedom, with grandeur shall rise,
  Unshaken by tyranny's blast;
Its basis the earth, and its summit the skies,
  And firm as creation shall last."

CHORUS.

Then rouse, fair Columbia, to glory aspire;
  All nature with transport shall gaze:
E'en now the dark shadows of discord retire,
  And Europe is lost in thy blaze.

GOD *save* great WASHINGTON.

TO Heaven's empyreal height
  Did ministers of light
      Their seats ascend;
A glorious Order shone
Around th' Almighty throne,
Who thus his will made known;
      Angels attend!

II.

Mankind on earth below
Shall more enlighten'd grow;
      Be this our care;

The world shall now be free,
Columbia, first to thee
We give the sacred tree;
   Preserve it fare.

III.

He ceas'd and shook the spheres;
With loud applauding cheers
   All nature rung:
Seraphs the concert join'd,
And heaven and earth combin'd,
And with enraptur'd mind
   His praises sung.

IV.

To guide us through the war,
Virginia's blazing star
   Beam'd bright its rays:
Tyrants beheld the sight,
And struck with wild affright,
Like the pale bird of night,
   In morning blaze.

V.

Discord abounds no more,
Nor leaves our fields in gore;
   She's broke her chains:
The gentle voice of peace
Bids all commotions cease,
And plenty's rich increase
   Adorns our plains.

VI.

O! may this fabric stand,
And may its name expand
   'Till nature dies:

When earth's majestic frame
Shall sink absorb'd in flame,
And Washington's bright fame
    To Heaven shall rise.

SONG.

COME, come, my friends, let's hail the day,
  That broke our chains, and set us free;
May all the nations quick advance,
And fix their rights, like us and France!

America was young and strong;
Not rich, but generous was the throng
Of free born lads, who flew to arms—
Ye despots say, has freedom charms?

They fought, they bled—sometimes were beat,
Yet never made a base retreat;
Let Trenton's streets, and Princeton prove
The force of Liberty and Love.

Our wifes, our children, left behind,
We grasp'd our arms, the foe to find:
And Brimus' heights, and Yorktown's field
May tell how mercenaries yield.

Fill up the glasses, toast to France,
May she to strength and fame advance;
May commerce all her store increase,
And all her struggles end in peace.

ODE TO PEACE.

COME, peace of mind, delightful guest!
  Return, and make thy downy nest
  Once more in this sad heart:

Nor riches I, nor pow'r pursue,
Nor hold forbidden joys in view,
   We, therefore, need not part.

Where wilt thou dwell, if not with me,
From av'rice and ambition free,
   And pleasure's fatal wiles?
For whom, alas! dost thou prepare
The sweets that I was wont to share,
   The banquet of thy smiles?

The great, the gay, shall they partake
The heav'n alone that thou canst make?
   And wilt thou quit the stream
That murmurs through the dewy mead,
The grove and the sequester'd shed,
   To be a guest with them?

For thee I panted, thee I priz'd
For thee I gladly sacrific'd
   Whate'er I lov'd before;
And shall I see thee start away,
And helpless, hopeless, hear thee say,
   " Farewell, we meet no more!"

A NEW SONG.

I.

WHILST sycophantic trembling slaves
   To despots bend the knee,
Fair Gallia ev'ry danger braves,
   Determin'd to be free.
With eager joy, her sons we meet,
   To take them by the hand;
For Freedom's sons, in ev'ry clime,
   Will by each other stand.

II.

With smiles by some you'll be receiv'd,
    Whilst in prosperity;
But gallant friends! be not deceiv'd
    By foul hypocrisy.
Trust none but those who've steadily
    Held forth a friendly hand;
Such men (let fortune smile or frown)
    Will by each other stand.

III.

What! tho' oppression's imps may join
    Your freedom to annoy;
What! tho' tyrannic friends combine
    That freedom to destroy:
Yet shall celestial Liberty
    Conduct you by the hand,
And Democratic Citizens
    Will by each other stand.

IV.

Against those execrable foes
    Destruction shall be hurl'd;
And may your salutary blows
    Regenerate the world;
Then shall our two Republics firm,
    United hand in hand,
Progress towards eternity,
    And by each other stand.

V.

Your efforts crown'd with victory,
    Despots are trembling seen!
And may each tyrant speedily
    Obtain a guillotine;

Then shall fair Peace, with Liberty,
    Close joining hand in hand,
Succeed to war, and discord fell,
    And by each other stand.

ODE,

On the FOURTEENTH of JULY.

THE red arm of slaughter is stretch'd o'er the plain,
But Liberty springs from the blood of the slain;
Base tyranny trembles, and cruelty fails,
As bright to the world she her standard unveils;
To the earth's utmost verge shall her power extend,
And her smile the hard reign of oppression shall end.

On this day remember the black fabric* fell,
By tyrants invented, curst emblem of hell;
Where hid from the light, and confin'd from the air,
Consum'd the pale victims of frantic despair;
Where anguish, unpitied, was heard to complain,
And innocence suffer'd the wheel and the chain.

'Tis past, and on adament records shall stand
The day that shed light on the gloom of the land,
While gratitude loudly to fame shall proclaim,
With heart proudly swelling, each patriot name,
Who, fearless of danger, rush'd on to secure
That Freedom which Heaven decrees shall endure.

Who fall in this cause, are translated on high,
Where glory prepares them rewards in the sky;

* *The Bastile.*

S

The turf which enwraps them, shall oft be bedew'd
With the tears of the beauteous, the brave, and
    the good;
Sensibility breathing her incense divine,
Round their urns shall th' laurel unfading entwine.

Thy cause, sacred freedom, shall ever succeed,
While patriots have bosoms to feel and to bleed;
Not a tear-drop for self shall e'er rush to their eye,
For their Country they fight, and for Liberty die;
Pursue then, ye heroes, the glorious plan,
Which gives to the People the true Rights of Man.

AN ODE.

Tune—The Hero comes.

WHEN first the mitre's wrath to shun,
    Our grandsires travell'd with the sun,
Columbia's wilds they sought from far,
And Freedom shone their guiding star.
  Freedom, &c.

CHORUS.

    Seize thy clarion, fame,
    Let the poles proclaim
    Each illustrious name
        That cross'd the pathless wave;
    Join, ye martial throng,
    Fame's immortal song,
    Bid the chorus roll along,
        Long live the brave.

In battle brave, in council wise,
They bade the school of valour rise,
Whose pupils aw'd th' astonish'd world,
And Freedom's sacred flag unfurl'd.
  Freedom's, &c.

CHORUS.

Seize thy clarion, fame,
Let the poles proclaim
Each illustrious name
   That bade these banners wave;
Join, &c.

While o'er our fields with havoc dy'd,
Bellona roll'd her crimson tide,
Like beauty's lovely goddess, rose
Bright Freedom, from our sea of woes.
  Freedom, &c.

CHORUS.

Seize thy clarion, fame,
Let the poles proclaim
Every Hero's name,
   That dar'd our rights to save;
Join, &c.

Well skill'd to guide the helm of state,
Like Howard good, like Chatham great,
A chief was ours, of deathless fame,
And Hancock was the god-like name.
  Hancock, &c.

CHORUS.

Seize thy clarion, fame,
Let the poles proclaim
Hancock's glorious name,
   Whose soul disdain'd the slave;
Join, &c.

Columbia wept—the Virtues sigh'd—
And Freedom mourn'd when Hancock died;
While choirs of Seraphs sung on high,
He's welcome to his native sky.
    Welcome, &c.

CHORUS.

Seize thy clarion, fame,
Let the poles proclaim,
Hancock's deathless name
   Has triumph'd o'er the grave;
Join, &c.

To arms! to arms! when Freedom calls,
No pang the Hero's breast appals;
But when the trumpet's clangours cease,
Let Virtue tune the lute of peace.
  Virtue, &c.

CHORUS.

Seize thy clarion, fame,
Let the poles proclaim,
Freedom's glorious flame
   Shall soon inspire the slave;
Join, ye martial throng,
Fame's immortal song,
Bid the chorus roll along,
   Long live the brave!

ODE TO TYRANTS.

Peter Pindar, with his poetical broomstick, belaboreth foreign tyrants—Taketh the part of the oppressed poor—Asketh tyrants knotty and puzzling questions—Giveth a speech of Cato—Peter seriously informeth them that they are not like the Lord—Peter taketh a survey of the furniture of their heads—Peter solemnly declareth that the million doth not like to be ridden—Giveth an insolent speech of tyrants, and calleth them highwaymen—The Taylor and the satin breeches—The Shoe maker and the shoes—Peter lamenteth that there should be some who think it a sin to resist tyrants—Adviseth them to read Æsop's fables.

WHO, and what are you, sceptred bullies?—
  speak;
That millions to your will must bow the neck,
  And, ox-like, meanly take the galling yoke?

Philosophers, your ignorance despise;
E'en folly, laughing, lifts her maudlin eyes,
   And freely on your wisdom cracks her joke.

How dare you on the men of labor tread,
Whose honest toils supply your mouths with bread:
Who, groaning, sweating, like so many hacks,
Work you the very cloaths upon your backs?
      Cloaths of calamity, I fear,
      That hold in ev'ry stitch a tear.

Who sent you?—Not the Lord who rules on high,
Sent you to man on purpose from the sky,
   Because of wisdom it is not a proof;
Show your credentials, Sirs: if you refuse,
Terrific gentlemen, our smiles excuse,
   Belief most certainly will keep aloof.

Old virtuous rugged Cato, on a day,
Thus to the soothsayers was heard to say,
" Augurs! by all the Gods it is shame
   To gull the mole-ey'd million at this rate;
Making of gaping blockheads such a game,
   Pretending to be hand and glove with fate!
On guts and garbage when ye meet,
To carry on the holy cheat,
How is it ye preserve that solemn grace,
Nor burst with laughter in each other's face?"

Thus to your courtiers, Sirs, might I exclaim,
   " In wonder's name,
How can ye meanly grov'ling bow the head,
   To pieces of gilt ginger-bread,
Fetch, carry, fawn, kneel, flatter, crawl, tell lies,
To please the creature that ye should despise?"

Tyrants, with all your pow'r and wide dominion,
Ye ar'n't a whit like God, in my opinion;
   Though you think otherwise, I do presume;

Hot to the marrow with the ruling luſt,
Fancying your crouching ſubjects ſo much duſt,
Your lofty ſelves the mighty ſweeping broom.

Open the warehouſes of all your brains;
Come, Sirs, turn out—let's ſee what each contains;
 Heav'ns how ridiculous! what motley ſtuff!
Shut, quickly ſhut again the brazen doors;
Too much of balderdaſh the eye explores;
 Yes, ſhut them, ſhut them, we have ſeen enough.

Are theſe the beings to beſtride a world?
To ſuch ſad beaſts, has God his creatures hurl'd?

Men want not tyrants—overbearing knaves;
Deſpots that wiſh to rule a realm of ſlaves;
 Proud to be gaz'd at by a reptile race:
Charm'd with the muſic of their clanking chains,
Pleas'd with the fog of ſtate that clouds their brains,
 Who cry with all the impudence of face,
"Behold your gods!—down raſcals on your knees;
 Your money, miſcreants—quick, no words, no
  ſtrife;
Your lands too, ſcoundrels, vermin, lice, bugs,
  fleas;
 And thank our mercy that allows you life!"

Thus ſpeaks the *highwayman* in purple pride,
On ſlavery's poor gall'd back ſo wont to ride.

Who would not laugh to ſee a taylor bow
 Submiſſive to a pair of ſatin breeches?
Saying, "O breeches, all men muſt allow
 There's ſomething in your aſpect that bewitches!

"Let me admire you, breeches, crown'd with
  glory;
And though I made you, let me ſtill adore ye:
Though a rump's humble ſervant, form'd for need,
 To keep it warm, yet, Lord! you are ſo fine,

I cannot think you are my work indeed—
 Though merely mortal, lo, you seem divine!"
Who would not quick exclaim, "the taylor's mad?"
Yet tyrant adoration is as bad.

See! Crispin make a pair of handsome shoes,
Silk and bespangled, such as ladies use—
 Suppose the shoes so proud, upon each heel,
Perk it in Crispin's face, with saucy pride,
And all the meanness of his trade deride,
 And all the state of self-importance feel;

Tell him the distance between them and him;
Crispin would quickly cry, " a pretty whim!
 "Confound your little bodies, though so fine,
Is not the silk and spangles that ye boast,
Put on you at my proper cost?
 Whatever's on ye, is it not all mine?
Did not I put you thus together pray?"
What could the simple shoes in answer say?

There too are some (thank Heaven they do not
 swarm)
Who deem it foul to stay a tyrant's arm,
 That falls with fate upon their humble sculls;
Some for a despot's rod have heav'd a sigh!
Let such on wiser Æsop cast an eye,
 And read the fable of the frogs—the fools.

Burke's *Address to the* SWINISH* MULTITUDE.
 Tune—Derry Down, &c.

YE vile swinish herd in the sty of taxation,
 What would you be after? disturbing the
 nation:

 * The following passage is extracted verbatum
from Mr. Burke's reflections on the French Revolution, page 117—" Along with its natural protectors and guardians, learning will be cast into the mire, and trodden under the hoofs of a swinish multitude."

Give over your grunting, be off to your sty,
Nor dare to look up, if a king passes by.
 Get you down! down! down! keep you down.

Do you know what a king is? by Patrick I'll tell you—
He has power in his pocket to buy and to sell you,
To make you all soldiers, or keep you at work,
To hang you, and cure you for ham or salt pork.
 Get you down, &c.

Do you think a king is no more than a man?
Ye brutish, ye swinish, irrational clan;
I swear by his office, his right is divine,
To flog you, and feed you, and treat you like swine.
 Get you down, &c.

To be sure I have said (but I spoke it abrupt)
That the state is defective, and also corrupt;
Yet remember I told you, with caution to peep
(For swine at a distance we prudently keep.)
 Get you down, &c.

Now the church and the state, to keep each other warm,
Are married together, and where is the harm?
How healthy and wealthy are husband and wife!
But swine are excluded the conjugal life.
 Get you down, &c.

The state, it is true, have grown fat upon swine,
And church's weak stomach on tithe pig can dine;
But neither, you know, as they roast at the fire,
Have a right to find fault with the cooks, or inquire.
 Get you down, &c.

What use do we make of your money, you say?
Why, the first law of nature—we take our own pay,

And next on our friends a few penfions beftow,
And to you we apply, when our treafures run low.
    Get you down, &c.

Confider our boroughs, ye grumbling fwine,
At corruption and taxes they never repine;
If we only proclaim, "Ye are happy"—they fay,
"We are happy"—believe, and be happy as they.
    Get you down, &c.

What know ye of commons, of kings, or of lords,
But what the dim light of taxation affords?
Be contented with that—and no more of your rout,
Or a new proclamation fhall muzzle your fnout.
    Get you down, &c.

And now for the fun, or the light of the day,
"It does not belong to a Pitt," you will fay:
I tell you be filent, and hufh all your jars,
Or he'll charge you a farthing a piece for the ftars.
    Get you down, &c.

Here's myfelf, and his Darknefs, and Henry Dundafs,
Scotch, Englifh, and Irifh, with fronts made of brafs;
A cord platted threefold, will ftand a good pull,
Againft Sawney and Patrick, and Old Johnny Bull.
    Get you down, &c.

To conclude—then no more about man and his rights,
Tom Paine, and a rabble of liberty lights,
That you are but our fwine, if ye ever forget,
We'll throw you alive to the horrible Pitt.
    Get you down, &c.

CHARMING KITTY.

THO' many a nymph may claim my song,
    For shape and grace, and feature handsome;
Yet, Kate, such charms to thee belong,
    As well are worth a monarch's ransom:
And had I India's wealth in store,
    I'd shun with joy the court or city;
And live sequester'd evermore
    With thee, sweet maid, my charming Kitty.

I many an acre, Kate, can boast,
    Large tracts of land, and golden treasure;
Then come, sweet girl, I love thee most,
    I'll lay it at thy feet with pleasure.
For thee I'll e'en the sex resign—
    The fair, the brown, the gay, the witty;
If thou'lt be mine, and only mine,
    Sweet rustic maid, my charming Kitty.

Then leave the shepherds, bonny Kate;
    Lay by thy crook, each care give over;
And let me henceforth on thee wait,
    A task, how pleasing to a Lover!
My life I'll dedicate to thee,
    And sing thee oft a tender ditty,
If thou'lt consent to live with me,
    Sweet rustic maid, my charming Kitty.

On BEAUTY.

EXULTING Beauty! phantom of an hour!
    Whose magic spells enchain the heart;
Ah! what avails thy fascinating power,
Thy thrilling smile, thy witching art?
Soon as thy radiant form is seen,
Thy native grace, thy timid mien,
Thy hour is past—thy charms are vain;
Pale Envy haunts thee with her meagre train,

Delusive Flattery cheats thy list'ning ear,
And Slander stains thy cheek with Sorrow's bitter tear.
  So have I seen an infant flow'r
  Bespangled o'er with silv'ry dew,
  At purple dawn's refreshing hour
  Glow with warm tints of *Tyrian* hue.
Beneath an aged oak's wide-spreading shade,
Where no rude winds, or beating storms invade:
  Transplanted from its lonely bed,
  No more it scatters sweets around,
  No more it rears its fragrant head,
  No more its sparkling tears begem the ground:
For ah! the beauteous flow'r, too soon
Scorch'd by the burning glare of day,
Faints, at the sultry glow of noon,
Droops its enamel'd head——and, blushing, dies away.

A SONG,

Written at an Inn at Henley.

TO thee, fair freedom, I retire,
    From flattery, cards, and dice and din;
Nor art thou found in mansions higher
    Than the low cot, or humble Inn.

'Tis here with boundless pow'r I reign,
    And ev'ry health which I begin,
Converts dull port to bright champagne,
    Such pleasure crowns it at an Inn.

I fly from pomp, I fly from plate,
    I fly from falshood's specious grin,
Freedom I love, and form I hate,
    And choose my lodgings at an Inn:

Here waiter, take my sordid ore,
  Which lacqueys else might hope to win;
It buys what kings have not in store,
  It buys me pleasure at an Inn.

Whoe'er has travell'd life's dull round,
  Where'er his stages may have been,
May sigh to think he still has found
  The warmest welcome at an Inn.

LINES,

From a disappointed Lover to his obdurate Mistress, after recovering from his paroxysm of Love.

AN angel of the darkest hue,
  Sent here from Satan's realm below,
Would torture less by far than you,
  Maria, author of my woe.

For you, by necromantick art,
  My soul did fill with dire despair;
Of vivid joy bereft my heart,
  And plac'd it in corroding care.

But now each charm, each winning grace,
  Which once my ravish'd soul did please,
And all the beauties of thy face,
  Have no effect—my mind's at ease.

No more on bended knee I crave
  On me to look with piteous eye;
No more I beg my life to save,
  No more shalt thou my suit deny.

For, on those sparkling eyes so black,
  And lips so sweet of rosy hue,
And breasts of snow, I've turn'd my back,
  Care not a fig for them or you.

HOPE.

WHEN stranded on some desart coast,
    Where hungry tygers roar,
The Sailor hopes—though all is lost,
    To reach his native shore.

The Captive in some prison drear,
    Opprest with grief and pain,
Still fondly hopes, the coming year,
    His freedom to retain.

The Lover, wretched and forlorn,
    Who now dejected roves,
Yet hopes, on some auspicious morn,
    To gain the Maid he loves.

Thus Hope, thro' life, enchanting pow'r!
    Enlivens ev'ry breast;
And ev'n in Death's terrific hour,
    Beguiles the soul to rest.

A NEW SONG.

PRAY kiss me, gentle Chloe cry'd,
    For I am weak and tender!
I will, my dear, the Swain reply'd,
    Forbearing to offend her.

Then closely shutting both his lips,
    (Regarding well his honor)
Her rosy mouth he lightly sips,
    And fixt his eyes upon her.

" O fie! (says she) you make me blush,
    Be quick and have it over,

I would not give a single rush
  For such a teazing lover."

At length, instructed how to please,
  (Resolving not to mind her)
He prest her closer by degrees,
  And found the damsel kinder.

SONG.

AT THE CLOSE OF HARVEST.

WITH thankful hearts and cheerful voice,
  Let all the nymphs and swains rejoice,
    And singing merry make;
The plenteous harvest now secure,
Let old and young the pleasures pure
    Of rural life partake.

The barns now fill'd with hay and grain,
To spend when storms of snow and rain
    Wide devastation brings;
Each breast let gratitude possess,
Each willing soul forever bless
    The Giver of good things.

Set round the board like christian friends,
Let us partake what Heaven sends,
    The produce of the earth:
Let foreign spirits ne'er intrude,
To make us angry, rough, or rude,
    And poison all our mirth.

The jovial song and lively dance,
The joys of human life advance,
    Let no one then be sad;

Why with dull superstition's cloud,
Should we th' Almighty's image shroud,
   When scripture bids be glad?

Then let the hardy jovial swain,
That lately mow'd the flow'ry plain,
   Unbend himself awhile;
And Susan quit her spinning wheel,
And join to dance the country reel,
   Forgetting all her toil.

The contemplative mind of age,
And sedate philosophic sage,
   Will join the social band:
While music's most enchanting sound,
And joy and virtue dance around,
   Forever hand in hand.

The COQUETTE.

HAVE I then committed treason?
   Why does Celia pout and fret?
Damon sure you know the reason—
   Every beauty's a Coquette.

Why does Chloe scorn her lover,
   When my lord will flirting sit?
Sure 'tis easy to discover
   Pretty Chloe's a Coquette.

Sylvia lips and thinks it pretty,
   Ask her why, she's in a pet;
I grant you faith it is a pity,
   Yet Sylvia too is a Coquette.

Ancient Sylla borrows graces
   (Every charm long out of date)

Yet with youthful air she paces,
  And is still an old Coquette.

Lucia, long in anguish sighing,
  With the archer blind beset,
Wipes her eyes, forgets her crying,
  Passing now a grand Coquette.

Never wonder, gentle Damon,
  Pretty Celia's airs forget,
Tis inth yarn our only way, man;
  All exclaim she's a Coquette.

An ODE on MUSIC.

LET Music's sons rejoice,
  Her daughters join their voice,
      And all combine;
Music, enchanting name,
Thou doth our hearts inflame,
Thy praise we will proclaim
      In songs divine.

Music, thou pleasing theme,
On us thy beauties beam,
      And tune our lay;
Thou will the soul refine
To raptures all divine,
'Till we shall rise and shine
      In endless day.

Then do thou worthy Lamb,
Who did'st our souls redeem
      From burning pains,
Accept the songs we bring,
Thou dear Almighty King,
Thy praise we'll shout and sing
      In endless strains.

While in this dark abode,
Teach us, O God, the road
    To joys on high ;
There we'll our voices raise
In most enraptur'd lays ;
The loftiest note of praise
    Shall never die.

Dear Lamb, who once was slain,
With thee we'll live and reign
    To endless days ;
Music shall fill our tongue,
Angels assist the song,
While all the blissful throng
    Resound thy praise.

ADDRESS TO THE GODDESS OF LOVE.

THOU lovely daughter of the sea,
  Smile now propitious upon me,
    And dry this glist'ning tear ;
Quick do thou my fond suit convey,
With fairest flowers strew all the way
    To her I love most dear.

While Phoebus' aids buckle his car,
Steal softly from thy Sylvan war,
    And take a lover's part :
Send, send thy little boy before,
With darts and arrows in full store,
    To captivate her heart.

Let the sweet music of the grove,
With am'rous doves surround my love,
    To raise the flame of joy !

So shall I tread Elysian ground,
And ev'ry thing be rapture found,
All bliss without alloy.

DELIA—A SONG.

DELIA, for thee I'd seek the fire
  Of millions 'volv'd in deadly war;
Nor from the field would I retire,
  'Till death or vict'ry crown'd my car.
    Tho' cannons found,
    And balls rebound;
    Tho' helmets meet,
    And troops retreat,

It should within no tremors raise,
  No sigh should draw, no tear should cause,
But in the sun's all parching blaze
  I'd wield my sword, and seek applause;
    Tho' Heaven's high arch,
    Deep veil'd, and dark
    With thunder roar'd,
    And lightning shower'd,

I'd firm remain amidst the field,
  Wide o'er the plain pursue my foe;
'Till in the combat he should yield,
  Or strike the last decisive blow.
    If she approv'd,
    She whom I lov'd,
    For one kind smile
    Would pay my toil.

Young Cupid has so aim'd his dart,
  And Delia so impress'd my soul,
That I've resign'd to her my heart,
  For she alone can bear controul,

So life's a jest,
A plague at best,
Unless she'll prove
A friend to love.

Her voice can sooth the sound of death,
　Can rob the grave of ev'ry ill.
Like Hermon's dew descends her breath,
　And sweetens life's all pois'ning pill.
　　　Delia, be kind,
　　　For I'm resign'd
　　　To gloomy care
　　　And wild despair.

To the cold mansions of the tomb,
　For I can bear misfortune's frown,
And all the ills of life to come,
　If you will but the Stranger own.
　　　If you will rove
　　　To Hymen's grove,
　　　And heart with hand
　　　Confirm the band.

AN ODE,

For the FOURTH *of* JULY.

HAIL lovely maid! Hail power divine!
　Hail *Independence!* at whose shrine
　　The just do tribute pay;
May thy bright rays each patriot fire,
May earth-born souls to thee aspire,
　　And hail th'auspicious Day.

On Europe's mystic shore enchain'd
By despots' mandates there restrain'd,
　　By superstition bound;

Columbus, like the orient morn,
Arose, dispell'd the black'ning storm,
    And leap'd the gulph profound.

The Curlew scream'd, the Tritons blew,
While cross th' Atlantic swift they flew,
    To reach Vespacia's clime ;
The sea-gods rose from ocean's bed,
The patriot band in safety led
    The radiant maid divine.

The Dryads hail their Heaven-born guest,
And Freedom rear'd its fulgent crest,
    And hail'd the auspicious rite ;
The clarions loud from state to state
Fair Independence verberate,
    When first she saw the light.

The mandates of great Jove's obey'd,
The wood-nymphs seize the infant maid,
    Like wisdom fair she stands ;
As rolling years matur'd her age,
With bold oppression she engag'd,
    And burst despotic bands.

This day, this blest propitious day,
The rolls of light she did display,
    Asserted Freedom's cause ;
She broke tyrannic Albion's chain,
And drove him from fair truth's domain,
    Where nature's God forms laws.

Then, patriots, join the festive throng,
And hail this day with mirth and song,
    And harmony and glee ;
With shouts of joy from state to state,
Let Heaven's bright spheres reverberate
    IMMORTAL LIBERTY.

COLUMBIAN SONGSTER.

A SONG,

For the FOURTH of JULY.

[Tune—Yankee Doodle.]

WHEN Freedom's sons, at Heav'n's command,
  Shook off the British nation,
America did then assume
  An independent station.
The Congress then were men of sense,
  And truly patriotic!
They swore they would not pay their pence
  To any king despotic.

CHORUS.

And this the law of seventy-six,
  We swear each to maintain, sir,
No such vile things, as lords or kings,
  Shall in America reign, sir.

The laws they made were quick obey'd,
  Whigs vied with whigs for glory;
And Jack Burgoyne, like creeping Ned,
  Went home to tell his story.
At Bunker's Hill—Howe had his fill,
  His troops were mow'd down, sir,
While Gage, poor soul! who lov'd bones whole,
  'Fraid to quit the town, sir.
                And this the law, &c.

Cornwallis next, like frighted mole,
  At York Town burrow'd deep, sir,
But Washington, with bombs and gun,
  Soon rous'd him from his sleep, sir.
He made them prance a Yankee dance,
  Whilst martial music sounded,
Lay down their arms, five hundred score,
  By rebel troops surrounded.
                And this the law, &c.

Then straight they flew, to George their king,
    And told the doleful tale, sir,
How th' rebels swarm'd throughout the land,
    And cover'd hill ahd dale, sir.
His courtiers too, did round him throng,
    And all to make him easy;
No consolation cou'd afford,
    Alas! it drove him crazy.
                And this the law, &c.

And now, behold! he's vengeful frown,
    Brimful of wrath and chagrin;
Keeps western posts, and takes our ships,
    And won't stand to his bargain.
Then let's unite, assert our right,
    Thrash his majestic back, sir,
Starve all their isles, confound their wiles,
    And turn up t'other Jack, sir.
                And this the law, &c.

Whole hosts of priests and kings combin'd,
    (For their own preservation)
With gogs and magogs, emp'ror too,
    A pretty combination!
☞ But Frenchmen they, march brisk away,
    And shoot, and slash, and score 'em,
Ca ira sing, and Marsel'ois hymn,
    And bayonet all before them.
                And this the law, &c.

The Duke of York—light as a cork,
    In' letter 'o his pappy,
" My grenadiers have beat monsieurs,
    And made me truly happy!
Then pappy banish all your fears,
    I've made this protestation,
To fight it out, and bring about
    Their total extirpation."
                And this the law, &c.

" Our loſs is ſmall, ſcarce none at all,
　　Compar'd with th' en'mies loſſes,
We've loſt, big, little, great and ſmall,
　　Three men, two hundred horſes.
I cou'd do no leſs, than ſend expreſs
　　(For vict'ry always pleaſes)
I've tak'n a town—it's all my own,
　　The French call it—Landrecies.
　　　　　　　And this the law, &c.

In vain the lion boaſts his ſtrength,
　　That none's ſo ſtrong as he, ſir,
For now, behold ! reverſe of fate !
　　Down his bended knee, ſir.
Thus fares it with thoſe tyrant ſouls !
　　Who th' rights of man oppoſe, ſir,
While 'gallic-cock pick'd out his eyes,
　　The ſnapper pinn'd his noſe, ſir.
　　　　　　　And this the law, &c.

Prophets of old, have long foretold,
　　And alſo Revelation,
Moſt clear point out, beyond a doubt,
　　Th' downfall of 'Britiſh nation.
For their Alpha and Omega,
　　Will ſure come to an end ſoon,
Give 'em a kick, and tell old Nick,
　　" Take crazy George"—his grand-ſon.

CHORUS.

　　And this the law of ſeventy-ſix,
　　　We ſwear each to maintain, ſir !
　　No ſuch vile things, as lords or kings,
　　　Shall in America reign, ſir.

AN ODE, *On the* PRESIDENT's BIRTH-DAY.

ENTHRON'D in weeds of ſtate,
　The Goddeſs, Fredom, ſate
　　Among her peers—

What valiant son, she cry'd,
Dare on war's tempest ride,
And check great Albion's pride
    Below the spheres?

No one, great Jove maintain'd,
In heav'nly armies train'd,
    Need wake alarms—
This Day an Hero's born,
The world's exalted Son,
His name is WASHINGTON,
    Expert in arms.

The Goddess saw below,
On Vernon's sky-wrapt brow,
    His noble form—
On light'nings fierce she sped,
And hover'd round his head,
Her beauteous crescent spread
    Before the storm.

Then trembling at the view,
His glit'ring sword he drew,
    With placid mein—
'Tis right! she said—stand forth,
The god-like son of earth,
I come to bless thy birth
    In climes serene.

With joy extatic crown'd,
He heard the silver sound,
    Awake! be free!
Then grasp'd his sword again,
Saw armies cross the main,
Usurp his native plain
    Of Liberty.

[By T. Paine, author of the Rights of Man, &c.]
THE GREAT REPUBLIC:
Or, the Land of Love and Liberty.
Tune, "RULE BRITANNIA."

HAIL! Great Republic of the world
    The rising empire of the West;
Where fam'd *Columbus*, with mighty mind inspir'd,
    Gave tortur'd Europe scenes of rest.
       Be thou for ever, for ever great and free,
       The land of Love and Liberty.

Beneath thy spreading mantling vine,
    Beside the flow'ry groves in spring:
And on thy lofty, thy lofty mountain's brow,
    May all thy sons and fair ones sing.
       Chorus, &c.

From thee may rudest nations learn,
    To prize the cause thy sons began;
From thee may future, may future tyrants know,
    That sacred are the Rights of Man.
       Chorus, &c.

From thee may hated discord fly,
    With all her dark, her gloomy train;
And o'er thy fertile, thy fertile wide domain,
    May everlasting friendship reign.
       Chorus, &c.

Of thee may lisping infancy,
    The pleasing, wond'rous story tell;
And patriot sages in venerable mood,
    Instruct the world to govern well.
       Chorus, &c.

Ye guardian Angels watch around,
    From harms protect the new born State;
And all ye friendly, ye friendly nations join,
    And thus salute the Child of Fate.
       Be thou for ever, for ever great and free,
       The land of Love and Liberty.

FREE AMERICA.

THAT seat of science Athens and earth's proud
    mistress Rome,
Where now are all their glories, we scarce can find their
    tomb;
Then guard your rights Americans, nor stoop to law-
    less sway,
Oppose, oppose, oppose, oppose, for North America.

Proud Albian bow'd to Cæsar, and numerous Lords
    before,
To Picts, to Danes, to Normans, and many masters
    more;
But we the bold Americans, ne'er yet have fall'n a
    prey,
Huzza, huzza, huzza, huzza, for free America.

God bless this maiden climate, and thro' her vast do-
    main,
May hosts of heroes cluster, who scorn to wear a
    chain;
And blast the venal sycophants, who dare our rights
    betray,
And shout, huzza, huzza, huzza, for free America.

HAIL AMERICA.

HAIL America hail, unrival'd in fame,
    Thy foes in confusion, turn pale at thy name;
On thy Rockrooted virtue, firmly seated sublime,
Below thee break harmless, the billows of Time.
May thy starry flag, waving, still glory pursue,
And freedom find ever, a guardian in you.

    Huzza, huzza, huzza, brave America,
        Whom Freedom secures;
The high car of crest-blazing glory is yours.

Let Spain boast the treasures, that grow in her mines,
Let Gallia rejoice in her Olives and Vines;
Let bright sparkling Jewels in India prevail,
Let thy odours, Arabia, diffuse in each Gale;
'Tis America only is bless'd with the Soil,
Where the fair fruits of Virtue and Liberty smile.
    Huzza, &c.
For the blessings of Freedom and Plenty are yours.

Our bosoms enraptur'd beat high at thy name,
Thy health is our transport, thy triumph our fame;
Like our Sires with our swords, we'll support thy re-
    nown,
What they bought with their blood we'll defend with
    our own.
Smile ye guardians of Freedom, while our sons implore,
That America may florish 'til time be no more.
    Huzza, &c.
For the blessings of freedom and valor are yours.

The muses to thee their glad tribute shall pay,
They flourish with freedom, with freedom decay;
Their harps faintly murmur and silently stand,
While the sword of oppression hangs over own land.
Can the Eagle soar freely, or dart like the wind,
When his limbs are oppress'd or his pinions confin'd.
    Huzza, &c.
For science and arts and fair freedom are yours.

Unsheath'd while the sword of oppression remains,
And the blood of our heroes still crimson the plains;
See America weaping exhort each brave son,
That their hearts, as their glory, might always be one,
'Tis the charter of freedom—attend to the call—
United we stand, divided we fall.
    Huzza, &c.
For Patriots, and Heroes, and Virtue are yours.

With Sweetness and beauty thy daughters shall rise,
With rose blooming cheeks and love languishing Eyes,
The graces and virtue solid comforts prepare,
For heroes deserving the first of the fair.
For to whom should the blessings of freedom descend,
But the sons of those sires who dar'd freedom defend.

www.ingramcontent.com/pod-product-compliance
Lightning Source LLC
Chambersburg PA
CBHW020826230426
43666CB00007B/1115